Receiving The Promise

The Spirit's Work of Conversion

Thomas Weinandy O.F.M. Cap.

*Scripture quotations in this publication
are taken from the Revised Standard
Version Bible, Catholic Edition.
Copyright © 1965 and 1966.*

Nihil Obstat
Rev. Peter Hocken
Censor Deputatus

Imprimatur
Rev. Msgr. Raymond J. Boland
Vicar General for the
Archdiocese of Washington
March 8, 1985

ISBN   0-932085-01-6

The Word Among Us Press
P.O. Box 3646
Washington, D.C. 20007

Contents

Preface

Conversion: The Heart Of The Church

THE CHURCH TODAY SPEAKS OUT CONCERNING MANY issues: marriage and family life, war and peace, poverty and racial discrimination, abortion and homosexuality. Indeed, the church has an obligation to speak the truth of the gospel in relation to such issues. The heart of the church's mission, however, goes deeper than these problems and concerns, and does so without minimizing their legitimacy.

The heart of the church's mission is conversion—conversion of every individual's heart and mind to God the Father, through Jesus Christ and by the power of the Holy Spirit. All of the problems facing the human race, all the evils that confront and attack the authentic hopes and desires of every nation and people, can ultimately be conquered only in the light of Jesus Christ. Only when nations and peoples come to conversion to the Lord Jesus will the chains of evil enslaving the world today be broken. Then will the Spirit's power to worship God, to love and live at peace within ourselves and with others be released upon the world.

The church, in proclaiming that its central task is the evangelization and conversion of peoples, recognizes that sin is the "original wound which is the root of all other

wounds" (Pope John Paul II, *On Reconciliation and Penance*, 3).
It likewise proclaims that this wound of sin can only be
healed through "the conversion of hearts and for the
reconciliation of people with God and with one another"
(*ibid*, 6). This is accomplished through faith in Jesus and his
redemptive death and resurrection.

This book attempts to present not the thought of one
man, the author, but rather the living experience of an
entire community of Christian people: the Mother of God
Community. Over the past seventeen years this Christian
Community, in the Northern Maryland suburbs of Washington, D.C., has witnessed the transforming power of the
Holy Spirit at work in the lives of people—families, married and single people, priests and religious. We hope that
many can share in what the Lord has taught us about the
new life to which he calls us. Each of us must, as St. Paul
declares, "receive the promise of the Holy Spirit" (Galatians 3:14). Be born of the Spirit. Each of us must be
reconciled to God through faith in Jesus Christ.

Feast of St. Thomas Aquinas
1985

Abbreviations

Ad Don.	*Ad Donatum (Letter to Donatus)*
Cat. Lect.	*Catechetical Lectures (of St. Cyril of Jerusalem)*
Conf.	*Confessions*
D.V.	*Dei Verbum*
De Bapt.	*De Baptismo*
De Con.	*De Concordia*
De Myst.	*De Mysteriis*
De Off. Min.	*De Officiis Ministrorum*
De Pecc. Merit.	*De Peccatorum Meritis et Remissione*
De Praedest. Sant.	*De Praedestinatione Sanctorum*
De Spir. et Lit.	*De Spiritu et Littera*
De Spir. Sanct.	*De Spiritu Sancto*
Denz.	*Enchiridion Symbolorum Definitionum Et Declarationum*
In Is.	*In Isaiam (Homilies on Isaiah)*
In Joh.	*In Johannem (Homilies on St. John's Gospel)*
In Ps.	*In Psalmos (Homilies on the Psalms)*
L.G.	*Lumen Gentium*
Myst. Cat.	*Mystagogical Catechesis*
Procat.	*Procatechesis*
S.C.	*Sacrosanctum Concilium*
Trad. Apos.	*The Apostolic Tradition*

Part I
Called
To New Life

Chapter One

Today's Need For Conversion

MANY PEOPLE TODAY ARE DISSATISFIED WITH THE present state of Christian life. Many, including religious leaders and laity, would agree that Christian moral values are rapidly deteriorating in our society. Some of the central mysteries of our faith, the incarnation and resurrection, for example, are questioned and even denied. It is important to realize that this situation of confusion and decay indicates a much deeper crisis. Something crucial to our faith is at issue— Christians, knowingly or unknowingly, are shedding their faith in Jesus Christ and his gospel way of life for secular principles and values.

Many of us are searching for answers or finding "answers" to the questions of life and its meaning in contemporary non-Christian philosophies, values and attitudes. We tend to base our lives, what is important to us and how we are to live, in these secular principles. This usually shows itself in frantic self-interest, greed and self-aggrandizement. "I" becomes the sole center of our lives and interests. Thus, the Christian way of life is being challenged and undermined. No longer is action founded upon our love for God and love for others, the two greatest commandments. The truths of the gospel are being washed from our consciousness and replaced by attitudes and lifestyles which are contrary, as St. Paul says, to leading "a life worthy of the calling" which we rightfully possess as Christians (Ephesians 4:1).

The present situation is complicated too by the residual appearance of Christianity which survives in our culture today. We still see churches in our cities and towns. Politicians and public figures continue to invoke God's name. People, for the most part, are civil with pleasing personalities. Economically, many can afford the "good life" portrayed in the media. Because of this, the need for conversion, or a return to real faith in Jesus is not clearly recognized. We forget that *no one is born a Christian*. We forget that everyone is called to be born anew by the power of the Holy Spirit. We become oblivious to our desperate need for the salvation of Jesus Christ.

In this opening chapter, we wish to examine briefly the spectrum of situations within Christianity today in which conversion or deeper conversion is a necessity. We hope to illustrate how each of us may be called to a more mature faith in Jesus and a firmer commitment to living the gospel. In more clearly recognizing the truth of our present state and the state of Christianity, we will more readily allow the Holy Spirit to act in our lives.

Unbelievers

At one end of the spectrum is the adult non-believer. Missionaries, sent to unconverted countries, are commissioned to proclaim the Gospel by the power of the Holy Spirit. They must fulfill their commission no matter what religion the inhabitants profess. All peoples—Moslems, Buddhists and Hindus, atheists—have the right and privilege to hear the good news that Jesus Christ is their Lord and Savior, and that the very Spirit of God can dwell within them if they repent and believe. Even Jews, who share a common heritage with Christians, and believe in the one true God, must come to know that their Messiah has come in the person of Jesus.

Many non-believers are also found in what had been previously characterized as Catholic or Christian countries. While Western societies, both in Europe and America, may have been founded on Christian principles, it is naive to think that these principles are still predominant, or that people within these societies are automatically Christian. Large segments of the population in America and Europe today are not Christian even if some trappings of Christianity are still present. Many persons, including some in prominent positions in society, are not Christians and might indeed be anti-Christian. This is obvious in the values and principles held by some politicians, as well as by what is taught to our children in schools and universities.

Within contemporary Western culture many individuals, especially adolescents, have never heard the gospel. They are completely ignorant of the Christian truths because no one has ever spoken the truths to them. Others have heard only a mutilated form of the gospel. They have designed a confused and ambiguous collage of "Christian" fragments either from school, the media or their families. Such fragments might be that "Christmas is a time for giving" or "Christians should care for people." Both statements are true, but they hardly represent the heart or the totality of the gospel. Christmas, for example, primarily commemorates the incarnation of Jesus and is not just learning how to be generous as Dicken's *A Christmas Carol* portrays. People may reject this version of Christianity, but what they have rejected is not the genuine gospel. Still others have heard the true gospel and the call

6

of Christ within them. Like the rich young man, however, they have rejected both, preferring the glory and riches this world offers (see Luke 18:18-25).

The Conversion
Of An Unbeliever

Two traits characterized my life before coming to know Jesus Christ. These were pride and a certain powerlessness, or hopelessness. I grew up in a family that was very independent and saw no need to attend church—I was taught to be willing always to help others, and never to admit that I had any need for help. I got married very early and at the outset, I was confident I could take on the world and win. As time went on and we had children, I began to doubt my capabilities. I found I didn't know how to care for my family, had no idea how to manage money, and didn't know how to respond to my wife, who was becoming increasingly isolated and depressed. Characteristically, I responded by helping others. I joined the rescue squad and increased my involvement in a local youth group. I thought people in those places looked up to me and I controlled the situation.

In the meantime, my wife had become involved with a local Christian group, and I began to see changes in her. I thought Christianity was great for her. After all, it was tailor-made for people who needed others to tell them what to do. As time passed, I saw that my initial opinion of Christianity was totally unfounded. My wife was growing in ways deeper than mere resolutions and self-discipline could account for. She was becoming happy, peaceful and confident in her actions, while I was becoming more and more unsure of myself, and feeling really hopeless about life. I know she prayed that I would come to share this new life with her.

After about three years, I began to attend the functions of her Christian group and was amazed at the love these people had for one another, at their joy and peace. Through weekly meetings, I became convinced that God is real. As I grew in knowledge of God's plan for me, I gradually saw many things that had to be changed. Rather than being depressed about the prospect of relating to my wife in new ways, of taking authority and responsibility for my children, of changing old sinful habits and ideas, I had confidence that the Lord would make the changes. He never burdened me with these things, but always poured out the grace of knowledge of his actions through prayer and through my new Christian friends. I began to be freed from the doubts, fears, and sin that had plagued me up to then. I began to experience the joy, faith and peace that I was seeing in others. Initially, I was overcome with the changes Jesus had brought about in me through the power of the Spirit, and very thankful to be freed from my former way of life.

As time passed, however, the emphasis shifted. Rather than seeing all these changes as meant primarily for my own good, I saw that God expected me to use them for his glory, and to build up the body of Christ here on earth. I remember that God gave me a scripture from John 15:16 when he began to show me my calling. It says, "It was not you who chose me, but I who chose you to go forth and bear fruit, fruit that will last."

Nominal Christians

Many persons who call themselves Christians today actually are not. They may, for example, have been raised in a Catholic family, yet they seldom or never go to Mass or even practice their faith, nor have they formally joined another religion. They are indifferent and apathetic. They refer to themselves as Christians because they perceive themselves as good and responsible people. In heart and mind, however, they more closely resemble non-believers than true Christians. Their lifestyle and values are visibly no different from those of non-believers. They have never come to true repentance for sin, or made a mature personal commitment to Jesus, and they have no real awareness of the life of the Holy Spirit within them. Pope Paul VI, well aware of this prevalent phenomenon, stated, "Today there is a very large number of baptized people who for the most part have not formally renounced their Baptism but who are entirely indifferent to it and not living in accordance with it" (*Ev. Nun.*, 56).

Regular Churchgoers

Further along the spectrum are believers who are regular churchgoers. They range from persons who fulfill the bare legal minimum to those who participate in church activities and programs. Catholics in the former category who are "merely practicing" are apt to be present at Sunday worship in a largely passive manner, and are probably anxious to leave as soon as possible. They have never properly understood nor truly welcomed the gospel. They may pray on occasion, usually when they are in a "crisis situation" in which they are no longer in control. Their faith is weak. Who Jesus is and the gift of his salvation mean little to them. They are likely to be unclear on Christian morals and values. Ordinarily, they recognize little need for repentance and rarely, if ever, go to confession. They find nothing in Jesus and the gospel that touches their lives, nor are they aware, usually, that this is not as it should be. The main difference between "merely practicing" and nominal Christians is that the latter do go to church and, by doing so, are exposed to the gospel.

Conversion Of
A Practicing Catholic

If someone had asked me seven years ago how I felt about my life, I would have said, "Things are fine. Everything is going well." If I had been asked to describe my relationship with God at that time, I would have replied, "Okay, I guess." The truth was, I had never thought too much about God, except when attending Mass on Sunday. After sixteen years of Catholic education, I was convinced I knew a lot about God, but he was still "God"—out there somewhere, remote, inaccessible, occasionally checking up on me. I sincerely believed that when I died, he would add up the "good" things I had done, and subtract the "bad" and, with luck, I would make it into heaven. I preferred not to think much about the whole prospect, and I figured my death was an eternity away.

My basic outlook was that "God helps those who help themselves" (which I mistakenly thought was a quote from Scripture), so I tried pretty hard to do the right thing (at least on the surface). I found life easier when I did the things I was expected to do, which made other people approve of me. I lived to make others proud of me, starting with my parents, then teachers, friends at school and finally my husband.

I am trying to paint a picture of a nice girl, educated in the basics of Christianity, concerned mostly with personal happiness and fulfillment. I definitely did not see myself as a sinner, and didn't understand what I had done that required Jesus to die on a cross for me. I also knew, in my more reflective moments, that I wasn't a "saint," but then who was? I drifted into the decision to take the middle of the road and do the things that all the normal, good people around me did.

In my search for fulfillment, I found I needed "just one more thing" to make me happy. First it was marriage, then a house, then a baby, then just one more baby. I lived my life in expectation of the next event, and a vague restlessness was always present. By the time I had two children, I felt the most fulfilling thing I could be was the perfect mother. I began by reading every book I could find on raising children (including *How To Father*), but much of the advice was conflicting, and I had no objective standard to measure it against. I tried to apply everything I read. Consequently, most days I felt rather guilty, wondering if I had been too strict or too lenient. I also transferred my own sense of restlessness to my children and felt I should constantly expose them to different stimuli, or they would be stunted. I was trapped in inconsistencies, plagued by the fear that somewhere out there was the perfect mother and I was missing the mark.

At this point in my life, I happened to attend an informal gathering of people who prayed together and shared their lives. I was curious to learn what went on there, but also skeptical. That night I heard a speaker talk about a God-shaped void in each one of us—a hole only the Lord could fill. I knew what he was talking about. In the weeks that followed, I was excited by the possibility that God could be real for me, that he could actually speak to me, yet I was also afraid that this new Christian life was something I wouldn't be able to live out.

One afternoon, when I went to get my infant daughter after her nap, I could see how glad she was to see me—all smiley and wiggly. Then I had the thought that God had been waiting for all eternity for me to smile at him like that—the smile of a child dependent on a parent. That was all he required of me. He wanted me to turn away from the sin and death of my former life. He wanted me to turn to him and acknowledge him as my Father. This didn't happen in a flash of lightning or a clap of thunder, but it was an assurance of God's love I had never had before. He was no longer "God," but "Father."

This was just the beginning. God the Father had revealed himself to me and wanted me to experience the love of his Son and the Holy Spirit. No longer was I a Catholic in name only, but I began to see the truth that Jesus and his salvation could be a living part of my life and the life of my family.

Dutiful Christians

Toward the other end of the spectrum from the unbeliever is the "dutiful Christian," who has a strong desire to serve God and to take full part in the life of the Church. Catholics in this category love the Mass, and probably attend. Vital signs of full conversion, however, such as truly sharing the gospel with others, are missing. They might go to confession regularly, but sin patterns in their lives can continue year after year. For example, they might have held resentments for years or allowed selfish concerns to outweigh caring for others. These are all indicators that something is amiss in their relationship to God. They fail to experience his love and forgiveness. They probably pray daily, but have little or no sense of coming into touch with the living God. They clearly have faith, but something is missing. That something is full conversion. They are called to a personal knowledge of Jesus and the power of his cross to change their lives.

Witness Of A Priest

For almost forty years, I've prayed Psalm 119, proclaiming with so many other members of the body of Christ: "Forever, O Lord, thy word is firmly fixed in the heavens, thy faithfulness endures to all generations." Because of his faithfulness, I can acknowledge my debt of gratitude for God's kindness and mercy. Despite years of faithful observance as a religious priest, I know that apart from God's kindness, I could well be cynical, bitter or just living on my own terms today.

The years after Vatican II were times of tension between the old and the new, between differing aspirations and openness to change. At that time, I was a member of a theology faculty and responsible for the formation of students during their years of study. For me, those years of the late 60's and early 70's did not hold much clarity or hope. The renewal of the Church was "in" but I saw our efforts at renewal producing division rather than unity, alienation rather than new life, individualism rather than brotherhood. I had no answers; I yearned for peace and wondered about the future. In the midst of all this, I prayed for the Lord's peace, which seemed so far from my life.

A longing to find God began to grow within me. I knew part of my emptiness was because God was far away. I thought, "If I could only find God, experience God." I did not know what finding God would mean, but still the longing continued.

During a retreat in preparation for Christmas 1973, I spent three days praying and fasting in solitude. Again the desire to find God was with me, yet looking back, how foolish I was to seek God according to my own academic methods and ways. Providentially, it had been suggested that I prepare for Christ's birth by simply examining my conscience on the question of "what pleased God about my life and what pleased me about it."

Those days alone brought me to see the reality of my own self-centeredness, even to the point of directing my life according to my own aspirations of success, recognition and satisfaction, and then asking God to bless the idol of my hands. By his grace, I repented and asked his forgiveness through the mercy of his Son. In that time of repentance, I found God's love and presence in a new way. "A broken and contrite heart, O God, thou wilt not despise" (Psalm 51:17). God's forgiveness, reconciliation and presence was with me. I knew that God had touched me and wanted me to redirect my life in submission to his gracious desires.

This experience of God's mercy and forgiveness gave me the courage to begin to follow the Lord in a new way. It gave me a desire to listen to the Lord's voice and follow him despite uncertainty about the future. I know that the Lord is faithful. During the past ten years, my life has dramatically changed. Instead of doubt, I have a certainty of God's presence and power in his church; hope has replaced dogged determination; repentance has overcome resentment and cynicism; and the praise of God has long removed my cry, "How can I find you, O Lord?" "Blessed be the God and Father of our Lord Jesus Christ, the Father of mercies and God of all comfort, who comforts us in all our affliction, so that we may be able to comfort those who are in any affliction, with the comfort with which we ourselves are comforted by God" (2 Corinthians 1:3).

Baptized Children

Also within the spectrum are baptized children growing up in a Christian family. Infant baptism was widespread in the first centuries of the church and had become the universal custom by the end of the fifth century. While the church acknowledges that baptism confers grace upon the infant—snatching the child from the grasp of Satan and placing it under the protection of Christ's body—it recognizes nonetheless that personal conversion is still necessary. Baptized children need to come to a mature repentance for sin and make an adult commitment to Jesus Christ as Lord and Savior.

Christian and Catholic parents must be clear about this need. Too often we assume that baptized children in a Christian family "naturally" become Christian. The experience of many contemporary Christian families, however, demonstrates that this is not true. Many parents find that their children tend, as they grow up, to reject Christian truths, practices and commandments. Often the parents themselves do not perceive the peril their children face. To protect against this situation, we must never presume that children are "good" or "doing fine," but rather, understand that they are sinners at the very depth of their being. Without realizing it, parents often recognize this fact. How often are parents embarrassed by the behavior of their children—their rebellious, arrogant behavior, "smart" remarks? These are but "signs" of their fallen condition.

In these situations, parents can see how much their children need Jesus and how much they must foster the truths of the faith even from infancy. The following witness gives a clear example of a baptized adolescent who came to definite knowledge of the truth of his faith.

Conversion Of A Baptized Adolescent

From my earliest years, I would have responded correctly to the question, "Who is Lord and Savior of the world?" In my Roman Catholic upbringing, I had been taught by my parents that Jesus Christ, the Son of God, God Himself, took on flesh and died for our sins. Our family of eleven often said the rosary together. Though this practice slowly disappeared from the family, church attendance never did. To this very day, my parents still go to daily Mass. They certainly taught their children the importance of the eucharist, and I followed their example by attending daily Mass for several years. I received a Catholic education from the parochial grade school and a Catholic Benedictine high school. I was confirmed, at age twelve, on the same day as my sister.

The fruit of my upbringing, however, was not evident in my life. Although I knew the right answers to questions, my knowledge was not a living reality. My participation in the sacraments was not bringing forth much life in me. Rather, I strived for other values commonly seen in the world today. Education was my greatest goal. I believed that if I received a Ph.D. from a reputable institution, I would be totally happy. My career would be set; my intelligence would gain me much prestige. This was a long-term goal. My short-term goals involved personal pleasures. I became more self-centered during my high school years, always wanting my own way. I grew more deceptive with my parents so that I could maintain my perfect image with them. At sixteen, sexuality and girlfriends, parties and drinking alcohol were prime concerns of mine. I also recall being with friends and thinking, "Why am I living? What is the purpose of life?" These are not the thoughts of one who knows the reality of Jesus Christ in his life.

Mercifully, Jesus opened my eyes that year to the truth of the Catholic faith. I heard the gospel that was preached to me by some Christian friends. I was convicted that I needed to repent of sin and give my life to Christ. Jesus had to change my life. I experienced conversion to Jesus Christ, who had previously been only a name, powerless to help me in daily struggles. I have no doubt that, before this time, I was like Lazarus in the tomb, both dead and bound. But Christ raised me to life when I was sixteen years old, so that I might serve his church, the body of Christ.

16

Receiving The Promise

The scriptures and the tradition of the church are now alive, bringing joy and excitement, and teaching me how Christ wants me to live. The Holy Spirit dwells within me, convicting me of sin and the righteousness of Jesus and empowering me to live according to God's commands. In my mid-twenties now, I am very grateful that Christ has raised me to life and allows me to serve him.

We have presented various situations in which people find themselves. Maybe you have already recognized yourself within the spectrum. To help you gain even deeper clarity, however, we now wish to ask a series of questions that will help discern the fruit of your faith, how alive it is, and how much it influences your daily life.

Questions Concerning Our Faith

- Do I confess on my lips that Jesus is Lord and believe in my heart that God raised him from the dead? (See Romans 10:9).
- Do I consistently experience the love of the Father and the power of the Holy Spirit? (The Spirit should enlighten us daily with his wisdom, knowledge and power to act as God wills.)
- Are my attitudes and life style motivated and governed by God's commands? Or, am I influenced by the standards of society in areas such as sexuality, marriage, wealth and status?
- Do I pray every day? Do I only ask God for things, or do I praise and thank Jesus for being Lord and Savior?
- Do I see my need to repent for sin, for example, for anger, jealousy, resentment and arrogance?

- Is my participation in the sacraments alive or just legalistic? Do I feel obligated to go to Mass but cannot wait to leave?
- Do I try to share my faith with others? (We only evangelize if our faith is alive. Otherwise, we will neither see the need nor have the desire to bring the good news to others, even members of our own families.)

Obviously, these questions can be amplified, but your answers to the ones above will give a fair indication of whether or not your faith in Jesus is alive, and the extent to which you need conversion. We all should recognize, however, that no matter how strong our faith is and how much we have grown spiritually, we are continually in need of conversion. We must examine, therefore, how we can come to a deeper faith in which the power of God's Spirit renews us.

Chapter Two
The Gospel
And Conversion

ANY SELF-EXAMINING CHRISTIAN CAN RECOGNIZE that deficiencies often exist in the way we live out the Christian life. We attempted to examine some of them in the first chapter, seeing that many of the values that motivate our lives are not truly Christian, but arise instead out of the secular culture of our day. Nonetheless, a clear-thinking Christian can distinguish between the true gospel of Christ and the principles of world-greed, self-aggrandizement, and self-interest.

In this chapter, the gospel will be presented in a clear, straightforward manner. In order to understand conversion and our absolute need for it, we must first learn God's plan for creation and the basic truths of the gospel. It would be well worth spending a little extra time in prayer and study. Read these pages carefully, since understanding and accepting this gospel can transform our lives and make us living Christians. Let us pray to the Holy Spirit, asking him to enlighten our understanding so that we might see the truth of the gospel. Let us pray that the Holy Spirit moves our wills so that we might give whole-hearted assent to what the Spirit teaches us.

God's Original Plan

Before the creation of the world, before time began, God existed as the Father, Son and Holy Spirit. As the Trinity of all-consuming life and infinite love, the Father, Son and Holy Spirit lacked nothing, but were complete and glorious in every way. Yet this Trinity of divine persons ordained to create, fashioning creatures after themselves, so that they might share in their own divine love and fellowship. In the infinite mind of God, who was without any need, the human race was conceived. The Father desired many sons and daughters who would be molded by the Holy Spirit into images of his powerful Son. What a prestigious and eminent position we human beings hold within creation! God "chose us in him [Christ] before the foundation of the world, that we should be holy and blameless before him. He destined us in love to be his sons through Jesus Christ . . ." (Ephesians 1:4-5).

Thus God's eternal desire was for each of us to know and love him in Christ. In knowing and loving God, we were to experience his infinite love for us. God would be our joy. So, at the appointed time, God created us in his very own image and likeness; he breathed his very own life-giving Spirit into us that we might have a special and intimate relationship with him (see Genesis 1:26-28, 2:7).

Genesis assures us of God's profound initial relationship of love with our first ancestors, Adam and Eve. He had placed them within the perfection of his creation (see Genesis 1:31, 2:15). He had created them as man and woman so that the two would be husband and wife, help-mates to each other who become one life-giving flesh (see Genesis 1:28, 2:18, 23-25). God intended that Adam and Eve would continue in his love. They were to live in perfect harmony with him and also live as one, caring for one another and for their kin. In this harmony, they would reflect their oneness with God and his protection of them. Their happiness, joy and peace would stem from knowing and experiencing God's love, and loving him and each other.

Arrogant Rebellion

We know that God's initial plan was thwarted by the sin of Adam and Eve. Their external disobedience to God's command reflected a deeper internal rebelliousness. They wanted to be like God himself, desiring to determine what was right and wrong, good and bad. They would not submit to God and his will. Rather, their own will would reign supreme (see Genesis 3:1-19). They willfully chose to live outside of God's authority and protection. They became independent of him. For human persons to be in such a condition is death itself.

By disobeying God's rightful authority through their arrogant rebellion, Adam and Eve were taking for themselves the supremacy God had intended for his Son Jesus, who was to be the center of creation. Everything was created for him. All of creation was to give him alone supreme honor and glory. Through their sin, Adam and Eve sought their own glory and prestige. All people have followed suit, usurping what alone belongs to Jesus (see Colossians 1:15-19).

Their arrogant rebellion devastated the goodness of God's entire creation. Such sin was an affront to the very love out of which God had created our first parents. The perversity of their sin was an insult to the holiness and authority of the almighty God. Adam and Eve no longer shared in a relationship of love with the Father: they were excluded from sharing in the life of the Trinity. Their sin had placed a gulf between themselves and God. Contrary to God's will, they had become his enemies, and even though God continued to love them, their hard and sinful hearts were impervious to his love. This was not an arbitrary punishment from God. It was the natural consequence of their seeking independence from him. Genesis portrays this disastrous situation as Adam and Eve hiding from God (see Genesis 3:8-10). They could not stand to be in his presence. Their sin had driven them out of the Garden (see Genesis 3:24). Fear, shame and guilt ruled their lives.

No One Seeks God

Not only were Adam and Eve alienated from God, but their own relationship was jeopardized. Neither took responsibility for this sin. Blaming one another and no longer at peace, they felt shame in each other's presence (see Genesis 3:7), and the unity of husband and wife, the order and love within human relationships, were now lost.

The rebelliousness of Adam and Eve affected all of human history. Because of the fall, we are born into a world of sin, death and separation from God. We participate by nature in this state of alienation and deprivation. St. Paul is emphatic on the basic human condition. In his letter to the Romans, he proclaims that both Jew and Greek fall under the wrath of God. Quoting Psalm 14, he states that all men and women are "under the power of sin, as it is written: 'None is righteous, no, not one; no one understands, no one seeks for God'" (Romans 3:9-10). He assures the world that "all have sinned and fall short of the glory of God" (Romans 3:23). This grave condition permeates the whole human race because "sin came into the world through one man and death through sin, and so death spread to all men because all men sinned" (Romans 5:12).

Our proper relationship with God is not the only thing sin has broken. We, like Adam and Eve, find that pride, rivalry and cunning rule our human relationships. Paul vividly describes life with one another in our fallen state, "Now the works of the flesh are plain: fornication, impurity, licentiousness, idolatry, sorcery, enmity, strife, jealousy, anger, selfishness, dissension, party spirit, envy, drunkenness, carousing, and the like" (Galatians 5:19-21). God had created us in his image and likeness so that we could love and care for one another, yet, we have turned our freedom to love into a weapon used to resent and hate.

The core of the problem lies within us. We cannot blame society or our upbringing, even though they both influence us. The hard truth is that each of us is a fallen and broken individual. We might know what we should and should not do, yet our pride and selfishness consistently rule our lives. Again, Paul expresses this truth with great clarity, "I do not understand my own actions. For I do not do what I want, but I do the very thing I hate. . . . For I do not do the good I want, but the evil I do not want is what I do" (Romans 7:15, 19). We should all be able to recognize the validity of Paul's words. In truth, before salvation in Christ, we are slaves to sin (see Romans 6:6, 7:14), easily ruled by our passions, emotions and uncontrolled desires. The hold sin has on us can easily be seen in our resentments and bitterness. If someone is unkind or unjust to us, or hurts us in some way, our *natural* reaction is to be bitter and to plot revenge. Only if we get control of our immediate and spontaneous anger, will we consider compassion and forgiveness. Even then, we find it very difficult to actually follow through and forgive someone.

Paul, however, does not despair, and we should not either. He concludes, "Wretched man that I am! Who will deliver me from this body of death? Thanks be to God through Jesus Christ our Lord!" (Romans 7:24-25). Christ is our hope.

The Immensity Of God's Love

In his gospel, John tells us, "God so loved the world that he gave his only Son, that whoever believes in him should not perish but have eternal life. For God sent his Son into the world, not to condemn the world, but that the world might be saved through him" (John 3:16-17). God's love is more powerful than the harsh reality of being independent from him. He sent his eternal Son into the world, as a man, to conquer Satan, destroy sin and vanquish death. Jesus is God's solution for man's slavery to sin, death and Satan. Jesus came into the world "to give his life as a ransom for many" (Mark 10:45).

Jesus' public ministry manifests the new life available in the kingdom of God. His exorcisms, healings and miracles demonstrate the power of the Spirit newly present to conquer Satan and all the effects of sin. His parables, forgiveness of sins and teaching with authority reveal the love and mercy of the Father. In these we see, in word and deed, the reality of God's kingdom breaking into the world. Through Christ, God is acting in a new way, and the power of his Spirit is changing people's lives. "In Christ God was reconciling the world to himself, not counting their trespasses against them . . ." (2 Corinthians 5:19). Through Christ, the hearts of men and women are being softened so as to accept his authority and salvation, and thus enter into the life of the Trinity.

God's love is revealed not only in the incarnation of his co-equal Son, but also in his Son's death and resurrection. Paul declares,

> . . . at the right time Christ died for the ungodly. Why, one will hardly die for a righteous man— though perhaps for a good man one will dare

24

even to die. But God shows his love for us in that
while we were yet sinners Christ died for us.

(Romans 5:6-8)

Jesus' death reconciled us to the Father. By offering himself on the cross, Jesus rectified the infinite wrong done to
almighty God, who loved his children as a true father, so
that the Father's love might be poured once more into our
hearts through the Holy Spirit (see Romans 5:5). "We have
peace with God through our Lord Jesus Christ" (Romans 5:1).

Jesus is God's justice given so that we might be just. "All
. . . are justified by his grace as a gift, through the redemption which is in Christ Jesus" (Romans 3:23). We have
been justified in his blood and "saved by him from the
wrath of God" (Romans 5:9). This is the good news of the
gospel. Jesus Christ died for our sins and his blood, the
blood of the eternal Son, has washed us clean of sin and
guilt. He has enabled us to stand justified and holy again
before God the Father. "In him we have redemption
through his blood, the forgiveness of our trespasses"
(Ephesians 1:7). The entire human race is now set right
with God.

Conversion: Born Of The Spirit

Conversion is entering the new reality of God's kingdom. We become new creations, born into a whole new
life, which we were entitled to from the foundation of the
world. We are cleansed in the blood of Christ and can lay
hold of the saving power of his glorious cross. Conversion
allows us to experience and participate in an entirely new
kind of relationship with God the Father, which brings
about a radical transformation within our own lives. This
new relationship is the work of the Holy Spirit. It is not
simply a part of being human. Jesus tells Nicodemus in

John's Gospel, "Truly, truly, I say to you, unless one is born of water and the Spirit, he cannot enter the kingdom of God. That which is born of the flesh is flesh, and that which is born of the Spirit is spirit" (John 3:5-6). As previously stated, no one is born a Christian—all begin human life separated from God. Each person, therefore, must enter into life with God through conversion.

The initial act of conversion comes by way of repentance and faith and we will examine these more closely later, after we state more fully the concrete effects of conversion in our lives.

St. Paul proclaims that through faith "God's love has been poured into our hearts through the Holy Spirit who has been given to us" (Romans 5:5). When we receive the Spirit we are empowered to know God as "Abba!, Father!" (see Romans 8:15). This new experience of God's love, this new relationship with him as an intimate Father, is unique to the Christian. Only those who participate in the salvation of Jesus Christ and who share in the life of his Spirit are incorporated into this relationship of love.

Life in the Spirit transforms us into new creations. Through conversion, we lay aside our former way of life and acquire "a fresh, spiritual way of thinking." We "put on the new nature created after the likeness of God in true righteousness and holiness" (Ephesians 4:22-24). As Christians, we are no longer enslaved by self-centeredness, arrogance and passion. Our minds become renewed by the truths of the gospel and the work of the Spirit. We come to think and act out of obedience to God and love for others and as the Spirit working within us transforms our minds, we grow more and more into the image of Christ. The fruit of the Spirit is love, joy, peace, patience, kindness, goodness, faithfulness, gentleness and self-control (see Galatians 5:22). Possessing the fruit of the Spirit is to live a life worthy of our calling as sons and daughters of God (see Ephesians 4:1).

New life in God's kingdom also assures us of our resurrection. Death has been conquered by the bodily resurrection of Jesus; his Spirit, dwelling in us, seals and guarantees our resurrection (see Ephesians 1:13-14). "If the Spirit of him who raised Jesus from the dead dwells in you, then he who raised Christ from the dead will bring your mortal bodies to life also, through the Spirit dwelling in you" (Romans 8:11).

The goal of conversion, of God's entire plan of salvation, is that all would come to glory in his Son (see Ephesians 1:10). Jesus, the glorious Lord of all history, will come again in the fullness of time, "after destroying every rule and every authority and power" (1 Corinthians 15:24). He will raise to eternal life and glory all those who have been faithful to him. "Then comes the end, when he delivers the kingdom to God the Father . . . that God may be everything to everyone" (1 Corinthians 15:24, 28).

This then is the whole purpose and primary end of conversion: to return us to God so we might live as one with him. From the beginning, God planned for each of us to live with him. Now, in order to return to God, we must turn away from sin, from our fallen Adam nature, and come to faith in Jesus through whom we have redemption, the forgiveness of our sin (see Ephesians 1:7-10). Repentance and faith are the conditions that God requires of us. God the Father has made Jesus our salvation, our way back to himself. In Jesus we have the fullness of life (see Ephesians 2:4-10).

We have presented the great truths and realities of the gospel of Jesus Christ. It is forthright and uncomplicated, yet profound and deep, and the basic truths can be easily stated:

- God, the Father, Son and Holy Spirit, existed from all eternity without need of any kind.
- God, out of love, created the world and formed human persons to share his life in Christ. God's desire was to have sons and daughters.
- The human race chose instead to live independent of God, cutting itself off from God's love and his divine life. Our lives became lives of sin and depravity.
- The Father sent his eternal Son into the world. Jesus became a man, suffered, died on the cross and rose. Thus, he rescued all people from eternal separation from God. Sin and death were conquered.
- Through repentance and faith in Jesus, the Holy Spirit is poured out into our lives once more giving us the dignity and privilege of being God's children. He is the guarantee of eternal life.
- In order to partake of this divine nature and share in the life of the Trinity, each of us must recognize our isolation from God and acknowledge our need for Jesus as Lord and Savior.

If we are to grow in faith and holiness, we ought to study and ponder these foundational truths prayerfully. Many of us have invested years in education and our professions so that we can gain knowledge and expertise. The more we learn the more we recognize how much is still unknown. Peculiar as it may seem, we do not put the same time and effort into our faith, and yet the "payoff" is of literally infinite value. We gloss over the gospel and wrongly assume we understand everything there is to know. The Holy Spirit wants to teach us so much more about the realities of our faith. He wants us to experience the depth of God's love, the forgiveness of our sin and the new life in Christ. The Holy Spirit wants to bring the gospel to life in our lives. If, as you read this chapter, your hearts began to burn with love for Jesus and you became joyful at hearing the good news, know that the Holy Spirit is working in your life right now!

Chapter Three

Only By
The Holy Spirit

THE HOLY SPIRIT IS THE BEGINNING AND END OF conversion. He is the catalyst in our lives that produces conversion, and is likewise the seal of it. The result of conversion is the indwelling of the Spirit through faith in Jesus Christ, which enables us to know God as Father.

Pope Paul VI, in his apostolic exhortation *Evangelii Nuntiandi* (1975) on Evangelization in the Modern World, recognized the supreme work of the Holy Spirit in conversion. "It is the Holy Spirit who explains to the faithful the deep meaning of the teaching of Jesus and his mystery." He "predisposes the soul of the hearer to be open and receptive to the Good News and to the Kingdom being proclaimed." The Holy Spirit "is the principal agent of evangelization." Moreover, "he is the goal of evangelization: he alone stirs up the new creation, the new humanity" (*Ev. Nun.*, 75).

In the 12th century, St. Anselm had also recognized the pervasive role of the Holy Spirit in the process of conversion. He stated, "Preaching is a grace, since what derives from grace is also a grace; and hearing is a grace, and the understanding which comes from hearing is a grace, and uprightness of willing is a grace" (*De Con.*, 3, 6). This understanding of the work of the Holy Spirit in conversion has not always been accepted. How and to what degree the Holy Spirit was active in the process of conversion became a controversial issue in the early fifth century.

Pelagius, an English monk, held that we could choose Christ and the gospel without the intervention of the Holy Spirit. Human freedom required no interior spiritual aid to accept the gospel. He saw insistence on the help of the Spirit to acquire faith as a denial of human freedom. For Pelagius, grace was made up of the gift of human freedom, the example and words of Christ, and the forgiveness of sin upon repentance. Repentance itself, faith and the living of a virtuous life were the sole work and responsibility of the believer. The Holy Spirit did nothing in our hearts to enable us to repent, believe and live a Christian life.

Augustine, the bishop of Hippo in North Africa, was the main opponent of Pelagius. He saw Pelagianism as an attack on the heart of the gospel. Salvation is a free gift from God that is wholly his work from beginning to end, and it cannot be merited in any way. Because of our fallen nature, the Spirit must work in our hearts and minds from the start if we are to come to faith and salvation. Pelagius never recognized the gravity and extent of the human fall. He believed we could equally choose good or evil, not realizing that once fallen, our hearts are bound by sin.

Augustine recognized that the work of the Spirit does not destroy human freedom. Rather, the Spirit breaks the bondage of sin, enabling us to choose Jesus freely as Lord and Savior. "Grace makes the will healthy so that by that will, righteousness may be freely loved" (*De Spir. et Lit.*, 52).

Later, a number of theologians in southern France, such as Cassian of Marseilles (c. 420) and Faustus of Riez (c. 470), proposed a theory that came to be known as Semi-Pelagianism. They admitted that the Spirit worked interiorly, but only after we took the first step towards God. Again, this doctrine attributed to us and not to the free gift of the Spirit the initial merit for our salvation.

The Council of Carthage in 418 condemned Pelagianism. Through the work of St. Fulgentius of Ruspe and St. Caesarius of Arles, the Council of Orange (529) condemned both Pelagianism and Semi-Pelagianism. The Council of Orange declared:

> If anyone says that mercy is divinely conferred upon us when, without God's grace, we believe, will, desire, strive, labor, pray, keep watch, study, beg, seek, knock for entrance, but does not profess that it is through the interior infusion and inspiration of the Holy Spirit that we believe, will, or are able to do all things in the way we ought; or if anyone grants that the help of grace is dependent upon humility of human obedience, and does not grant that it is the very gift of grace that makes us obedient and humble, he contradicts the words of the Apostle: "What have you that you did not receive?" (1 Corinthians 4:7); and "By the grace of God, I am what I am" (1 Corinthians 5:10).
>
> (*Denz.*, 376/179).

Most of us do not realize how our own conversion and our life of faith is so essentially intertwined with the work of the Holy Spirit. Often we can have the mind-set of Pelagius that, on a practical level, we alone, by our own mind and will, come to faith in God. We think this way because we see all "normal" events as purely the work and action of human beings, of human causality. In our culture, God is out to the side, and any claim of his action or intervention in the world is looked upon with suspicion.

Because of this attitude, we fail to recognize that faith is a work of the Holy Spirit within us, moving us to choose freely to believe in the Lord Jesus.

The work of faith then is dependent primarily upon God himself. Through the Holy Spirit, God the Father reveals his Son and the saving grace that comes through him to us. In Christ, the love of the Father is poured into our hearts. The Holy Spirit enlightens our minds so that we might recognize this work of God. Once we have perceived it, the Spirit moves our wills to give assent to what is revealed.

Obviously, however, our free act of belief is essential to faith. We do have to choose freely to acknowledge the truth of revelation. We do have to choose freely to believe, for we also have the ability to turn away from God and his grace. The act of faith always occurs within the context of God's revelation of himself to us accompanied by the action of the Holy Spirit within our hearts and minds. Faith is a sovereign act on our part, an inner consent to God, but this free human act cannot be accomplished apart from God's revelation.

What we can see here is the twofold aspect of faith. First, faith is God's work of revelation wrought in our lives by the Holy Spirit. Second, faith is our whole heartfelt assent to what God has done in Christ. Faith becomes the foundation of our continued daily interaction with God. In and through our life of faith, the Holy Spirit continues to act on behalf of God, and to nurture our free response to the Father.

Part II
The Elements Of Conversion

THUS FAR WE HAVE SEEN THAT EVERYONE NEEDS TO experience conversion (Chapter 1), that the goal of conversion is entrance into the life of the Father through Jesus Christ (Chapter 2) and that this relationship with the Father is entirely due to his mercy and love given to us through the Holy Spirit (Chapter 3). We wish to emphasize again that conversion is the work of the Trinity in our lives. We cooperate with the Spirit when we recognize the fact that at the heart of our existence we are at emnity with God and that we are in absolute need of the salvation the Father is offering us in Christ. Conversion culminates in our accepting by faith the gifts of salvation freely bestowed upon us. Our acceptance in faith grafts us to the very divine life of the Trinity.

Conversion then is not mysterious or strange. It cannot be. God has revealed to us the mystery, the plan, he decreed long ago. God chose each of us in Christ "before the foundation of the world, that we should be holy and blameless before him. He destined us in love to be his sons through Jesus Christ . . ." (Ephesians 1:4-5). This was God's gracious will and pleasure for each of us. Many of us, however, may experience God as far away or unknown, because in reality we have not come to the fullness of conversion. In conversion, we come to know God in a personal way, and the fulfillment of God's eternal plan in our own individual lives.

To help us understand conversion, this section presents the four elements of conversion: hearing the word of God, conviction of sin, repentance and faith. All four are essential for conversion to take place in our lives. In fact, full conversion can never take place without all of them. We must hear the gospel proclaimed, be convicted of sin, sincerely repent of the sin and come to personal faith in Jesus as Lord and Savior. These essential elements of conversion are brought about by the Holy Spirit's work within our lives. In adult non-believers, they lead up to and culminate in the sacraments of initiation: baptism, confirmation and the eucharist.

As you read further, keep in mind the basic situations in which all people need conversion. While only one group needs to be baptized (the unbaptized adult non-believers), the others, such as the non-practicing "Christian," the baptized child and the active churchgoer, need to come to true repentance and mature faith.

Chapter Four

Hearing The Proclamation Of The Gospel

S T. PAUL STATES THAT EVERY PERSON WHO CALLS UPON the Lord will be saved. "But how are men to call upon him in whom they have not believed? And how are they to believe in him of whom they have never hard? And how are they to hear without a preacher? And how can men preach unless they are sent? As it is written, "How beautiful are the feet of those who preach good news!" (Romans 10:14-15). Paul recognizes very clearly that the good news must be proclaimed, for only by its proclamation will we come to know the mighty works of God, and to participate in them through our new life in the Spirit. The primary task at the heart of the church's identity is to proclaim the gospel to every creature "that it may bring all men that light of Christ" (*L.G.* 1).

The Power Of The Gospel Proclaimed

We do wrong to underestimate the power of the gospel when it is proclaimed with clarity, conviction and the power of the Holy Spirit. By its very nature, God's word brings forth life when it is announced (see Isaiah 55:11), as Acts of the Apostles clearly demonstrates.

On Pentecost, for example, Peter simply and forthrightly salvation (see Acts 2:14-39). Later, he told Cornelius and his household that Jesus is the Lord of all and that he rose from the dead (see Acts 10:34-43). Even as Peter spoke, "The Holy Spirit fell on all who heard the word" (Acts 10:44). In the same way, Philip's proclamation to the Ethiopian eunuch exemplifies the power of the word. Responding to the eunuch's question concerning a scripture passage, "Philip opened his mouth and beginning with the scripture he told him the good news of Jesus" (Acts 8:35). Shortly afterwards the eunuch was baptized (see Acts 8:38).

These examples demonstrate that the Holy Spirit works in power when the gospel is proclaimed. The living truths of our faith and the words by which they are preached can penetrate the hardest of hearts and the darkest of minds: The Holy Spirit lies hidden in the gospel ready to spring into action as the word of God invades the ears and minds of its hearers, to bring forth light and life.

Thus, in situations where the gospel is truly preached, the Holy Spirit is dynamically active and anoints both the speaker's words and the listener. Through the empowered word, the Holy Spirit enkindles in us the ability to perceive and understand the spoken truth as we hear it. He enlightens our minds and touches our sin-ridden hearts so that we recognize, deep inside, the validity and glory of the gospel. The Holy Spirit then illuminates the soul so that we can give assent to the truth that is clearly seen. In so doing, the Holy Spirit begins to conceive and foster his new life within our very beings.

St. Bonaventure in his *Minor Life of St. Francis* describes how Francis' preaching pierced the hearts of unbelievers.

Like a second Elisha, Francis now began to take
up the defense of the truth, all inflamed as he

was with the fiery order of the Spirit of Christ
. . . His words were full of the power of the Holy
Spirit, never empty or ridiculous and they went
straight to the depths of the heart, so that his
hearers were astonished beyond measure and
hardened sinners were moved by their penetra-
ting power.

(*Ch. 3, 2*)

Reading God's Word
And Studying The
Truths Of The Faith

We have been stressing the power of the gospel to alter
lives. In the examples given, the hearts of people were
touched by the word of God and radically changed. Upon
hearing the word of God, they responded as the seed
which fell on good soil and brought forth grain (Matthew
13:8). Similarly, we need to do several practical things with
the word we have heard in order to cooperate with and
promote the work the Spirit has begun. We must read
scripture, study the truths of the faith, learn to pray and
experience Christian fellowship.

Paul writes to Timothy, "all scripture is inspired by God
and profitable for teaching, for reproof, for correction and
for training in righteousness, that the man of God may be
complete, equipped for every good work" (2 Timothy 3:16-
17). St. Jerome states, "Ignorance of the scriptures is
ignorance of Christ" (In *Is., Prol.*).

As God's word, scripture is fundamental for coming to
know the truth of the gospel. We have already said that
the preaching of the word involves the Holy Spirit acting
in the word proclaimed and in the heart of the hearer.

42

When we prayerfully read the bible, a similar interaction occurs between the work of the Spirit in the text and the presence of the same Spirit in us. Inspired by the Spirit, the truth of the scripture enters our minds and convicts us. As the letter to Timothy states, scripture is important both for coming to know the truth and for learning how Christians are to live. Many of Paul's letters are structured this way. The first part is a proclamation of Christian doctrine, and the second part is moral exhortation and teaching (for example, see Ephesians 1-3 and 4-6 or Galatians 1-4 and 5-6).

Whether an adult non-believer, a growing child, a nominal Christian or a practicing Christian, we need to read and study God's word if we are to come to a knowledge of Jesus and the gospel. Reading scripture renews our conviction.

Prayer for the Holy Spirit's light is essential when we read God's word. Only the Spirit can enlighten our minds to grasp the reality of what we read, because human intellect alone is unable to fathom the mysteries of God. The Fathers of Vatican II urge that "prayer should accompany the reading of sacred scripture, so that a dialogue takes place between God and man. For, 'we speak to him when we pray; we listen to him when we read the divine oracles'" (St. Ambrose, *De Off. Min.*, I, 20, 88; *D.V.*, 25).

It is a valuable practice to ask God questions when we are reading scripture, for the Holy Spirit will teach much to a person who thirsts for the knowledge of God with an open heart and active mind. For example, if we desire faith, or question whether faith in Jesus is valid, we should ask Jesus to reveal to us the truth and meaning of his incarnation, of his death on the cross and of his resurrection. In the same way, we can ask the Holy Spirit questions about all Christian doctrine. Only through prayer and concerted study will we come to know and experience the truth of God's revelation through Christ in the Spirit.

Reading and studying scripture and the doctrines of our faith also allow the Spirit to counteract and reconstruct our fallen nature's tendency to believe lies and pursue sin. Cyril of Jerusalem tells his adult catechism class, "Give your mind wholly to study, that it may forget base things" (*Procat.*, 16). Conversion requires a change in what we accept as true and in how our minds think and react. Only by reading and studying can conversion to God's truth take place in depth.

Learning to Pray

Continuing on this practical level, the seed of conversion can take root in our lives only if it is nurtured with prayer, the vehicle by which we open ourselves to the work of the Spirit. Through prayer, we put ourselves in the presence of God, and God is able to reveal himself and speak to us. In prayer, we can begin to experience the love of God, and come to know Jesus as our personal Lord and Savior. We are able to see our own sinful condition and the need for repentance. Moreover, in prayer we can appropriate God's forgiveness and cleansing from guilt.

Prayer is essential to conversion. If we do not learn how to pray, the gospel will ultimately remain mere history and theological theory. In prayer, the truths of the gospel take on concrete expression and reality.

St. Cyril knew this very well. He exhorted his catechumen class:

> Prepare your hearts for reception of doctrine, for fellowship in holy mysteries. Pray more frequently, that God may make you worthy of the heavenly mysteries. Cease not day or night, but when

sleep is banished from your eyes, then let your
mind be free for prayer.

(*Procat.*, 16)

We would like to present a simple basic structure for
personal prayer, stressing time and place. Each of us needs
to have a time set aside each day for prayer. This should be
"prime time," a time when we are alert and not trying to
do something else, like driving a car. The morning is probably the best time, either before going to work or after the
children are off to school or at play. We should allot at least
fifteen minutes for prayer though we would benefit much
more by spending twenty to thirty minutes a day. We
should also find a place that is fairly free of distractions like
noise from the television or the phone ringing.

What should we do during our prayer time? Call to
mind the basic facts of the gospel. God created us and he
loves us. We have sinned, but Jesus has come to save us
from our sin and has given us eternal life. Jesus now reigns
in glory and intercedes on our behalf. Jesus wants to pour
forth his Holy Spirit into our lives. He desires that we
share fully in the Spirit's gifts.

In recalling and enumerating these marvelous truths,
we can begin to praise and thank God for what he has
done for us. The eternal and all holy Trinity—Father, Son
and Holy Spirit—is worthy of our worship and adoration.
Praising God in our own words gives true glory and honor
to him; using Psalms of praise can greatly assist us in
praising God. He is pleased beyond our imagination.

We have already mentioned that during prayer we can
ask God questions about the doctrines of our faith or what
God wants to do in our own lives. He can answer us by
speaking within our minds, or through scripture or in the
words of a brother or sister. We must be expectant,

though, in order to hear God. He does want to teach us all, especially those people who desire conversion and a deeper life with him. During prayer, we can also know God's forgiveness and seek his help in overcoming patterns of sin in us—He has promised that we will experience his mercy and consolation. We can seek his wisdom for our own lives and the lives of our families. We can intercede for the salvation and needs of others. Since daily prayer and scripture reading are essential to conversion and our own on-going life with Christ, we would like to recommend an aid to prayer and scripture: *The Word Among Us* magazine.

Christian Fellowship

We have been stressing the ways that the gospel touches people's lives: reading scripture, praying and experiencing good Christian fellowship. To become a Christian is to become part of God's people, the church. Conversion is not just an individual matter, but the grafting of an individual into the living Body of Christ. Paul tells the Corinthians that "by one Spirit we were all baptized into one body . . . all were made to drink of one Spirit" (1 Corinthians 12:13). Without Christian friends, our faith in Christ can weaken when confronted by the daily pressures of the world—like immoral or manipulative business practices, backbiting or sexual promiscuity. Through Christian friends, we can see the gospel lived out and be encouraged to persevere in the Christian way of life. Through Christian fellowship, we can see that it is possible to have true joy and happiness with others without sinning. The book of Sirach describes a Christian friend as "a sturdy shelter" and an "elixir of life." "He that has found one [a Christian friend] has found a treasure . . . no scales can measure his excellence" (Sirach 6:14, 16).

As we close this chapter, ask yourself the following questions.

- Do I kneel before God the Father each day, asking him to reveal to me the truth of his Son's gospel?
- Have I asked God, through his Holy Spirit, for the gift of faith?
- When was the last time I allowed the Spirit to touch me during a homily, while reading scripture or during prayer?
- Do I value friendship with other Christians?

Chapter Five

Conviction Of Sin And Repentance

S T. PAUL DESCRIBES IN STRIKING DETAIL THE DIFFERENCE between living in God's kingdom and living outside of it. He differentiates between the works of the flesh and the works of the Spirit.

Now the works of the flesh are plain: fornication, impurity, licentiousness, idolatry, sorcery, enmity, strife, jealousy, anger, selfishness, dissension, party spirit, envy, drunkenness, carousing, and the like. I warn you, as I warned you before, that those who do such things shall not inherit the kingdom of God. But the fruit of the Spirit is love, joy, peace, patience, kindness, goodness, faithfulness, gentleness, self-control; against such there is no law.

(Galatians 5:19-23)

We may think, "Well, I am not an adulterer, nor do I murder, therefore I am not that bad." True, we might not have done such things, but Paul also mentions in the same quotation what might seem to us small sins such as jealousy, anger and selfishness. Though apparently small, these sins do have a very harmful effect on our lives.

A woman once witnessed that she had thought she and her husband had a very good marriage. They loved each other. They were faithful to each other. One day, her oldest daughter asked her, "Why do you and dad argue so much?" Those words touched her and, though she was angry at first, she saw the truth: their relationship was riddled with bickering, dissension, envy and strife. These "little" sins were eating away at the heart of their relationship and the life of their family. She and her husband began to work on this, repenting whenever they caught themselves bickering. In six months they had made great progress, but it had taken honesty, humility and the work of Spirit-filled repentance.

If we examine our attitudes, we also will find sin. Are we motivated by selfish concerns? Do we judge others? Do we harbor resentments and refuse to forgive others? How often are our minds dominated by sensual thoughts and fantasies? We even fail to recognize our need for God, believing we can live the normal course of our days without him. (This is utter arrogance on our part.) These and other similar attitudes point to real sin in our lives.

Sin, then, is the mark of living outside God's kingdom. It weakens our human relationships, destroys the life in the Spirit within us and disrupts our friendship with God. Christianity demands turning from sin, since the effects of sin separate us from God.

This chapter describes the sinful, broken nature each person has and the mighty work of repentance available through confession and deliverance. Be assured—only the Holy Spirit convicts us of sin and leads us to repentance. Human effort is not enough. Only the Spirit can help us in our struggle with the sin that enslaves us. We can cooperate with the Holy Spirit however, by examining our consciences daily.

Condition Of Mankind

Conviction of sin—one of the Holy Spirit's primary and essential tasks—is an absolutely sure sign of the Holy Spirit's work in our lives. Since he is the very holiness of God, the Spirit by nature brings to light whatever is not holy. Thus when we hear the gospel preached, the Spirit convicts us of our sinful condition.

Sin destroys the dignity of each person created in God's own image. When we hear the gospel, the Holy Spirit convicts us that we, like Adam, are in a state of arrogant rebellion against God and his commands. We see that we are in bondage to sin and evil. We grasp the truth of Paul's words that "sin reigns" in our lives (see Romans 6:12). We recognize that the Holy Spirit reveals, in contrast to our own sinful condition, the righteousness and holiness of Jesus in whom we must believe to receive forgiveness of sin. The ultimate rebellion is refusal to believe in Jesus and his righteousness (see John 16:8-9).

The Spirit not only illuminates the individual sins we have committed, but he reveals our true fallen state and participation in the sin of Adam. He enables us to recognize the truth that, at the heart of our being, we are sinners, shattered human beings in desperate need of healing and salvation. Through the light of the Spirit, we no longer pass sin off as the foibles and weaknesses inherent in the human species, but acknowledge it as a willed affront against the love and justice of God.

We are not the innocent, pleasant people we pretend to be, for the heart of a beast resides within us, full of malice and arrogance. St. John of Avila (1500-1569) describes the condition of all mankind:

> He who is in sin is less than a man. He is lost,
> made like a senseless beast, since he renounced
> grace and was disobedient to God. . . . So it is
> that because you abandoned God, not only were
> grace and virtue taken from you, but a beast's
> heart was given to you.
>
> *(The Holy Spirit, Sermon 5)*

When convicted of sin, we are confronted with a choice.
We can either say yes to the truth the Holy Spirit has
revealed to us, and then repent and believe in the saving
name of Jesus Christ, or we can reject the light of the
Spirit and refuse to repent and believe. There is no
ambiguity or confusion in our minds if we have truly been
convicted by the Holy Spirit. We see our state before God
in at least one particular area, and sense the hope that God
our loving Father is giving us. This is the work of the
Spirit who "will guide you into all the truth" (John 16:13).

The conviction is founded on God's word,

> [which is] living and active, sharper than any
> two-edged sword, piercing to the division of soul
> and spirit, of joints and marrow, and discerning
> the thoughts and intentions of the heart. And
> before him no creature is hidden, but all are open
> and laid bare to the eyes of him with whom we
> have to do.
>
> *(Hebrews 4:12-13)*

While the proper response is repentance and faith, the
opposite response is a real possibility. John's Gospel gives
the reason:

> And this is the judgment, that the light has come
> into the world, and men loved darkness rather

than light, because their deeds were evil. For every one who does evil hates the light, and does not come to the light, lest his deeds should be exposed. But he who does what is true comes to the light, that it may be clearly seen that his deeds have been wrought in God.

(John 3:19-21)

We can love darkness. We can refuse to change our evil lives, though refusal culminates in rejection of Jesus and his salvation. It becomes our own judgment upon ourselves. The Spirit has revealed the truth to us, and we have freely rejected it. Through the centuries, many people have realized that a stubborn refusal to repent and believe is "the sin against the Holy Spirit" (Matthew 12:32) which cannot be forgiven. They "perish because they refused to love the truth and so be saved" (2 Thessalonians 2:10).

The Spirit's conviction of sin is essential to conversion and we should not be frightened by it, no matter what our level of faith is. Since the convicting power of the Spirit brings with it a certain tension and even feelings of guilt, we can react against it and think that such "bad feelings" could not possibly be from an all-loving God.

The truth is, God does loves us—more than we can imagine—and he wants above all to heal and repair our lives. For him to do that, we cannot be left ignorant of our sinful state and our responsibility for it. We must see that we do need Jesus Christ. The Father sent his Son into the world out of love. He does not want to leave us where we are, but bring us from the hideousness of sin to the full joy of redemption. Playing down the reality of sin benefits no one and, instead, leads to building castles in the air— dreams that have no reality. Sin is an awful reality. It caused Jesus to die. But thanks be to God! Now the reality has been changed. We can escape the horror of sin and begin to appropriate an entirely new life in the Spirit.

When the Spirit convicts us and feelings of guilt well up within us, we should not become rebellious, defensive or eager to make excuses. Nor should we lash out at those who speak the truth to us, as if "they" made us feel guilty. The speaker-of-truth never makes us guilty. The Spirit, revealing the truth of our lives to our own consciences, causes guilt to rise up in us. We feel guilty because we *are* guilty! Yet we are not falsely accused. Recognition of guilt is not something to be loathed, no matter how bad we feel. Rather, to feel guilty is a true and valid work of God in our lives. The Holy Spirit does not convict us of sin so that we just feel guilty. No, he wants us to repent, to turn back to him. Unresolved guilt is an indication of unrepented sin. When we experience conviction of sin, we may emotionally feel guilty, but what we need to do is to *go beyond* the guilt to repentance. Jesus can remove our guilt, shame and embarrassment. He can forgive our sins. We can repent and become new creations.

Repentance

In recognizing the holiness of Jesus and the truth about himself, Peter falls down before him and says, "Depart from me, for I am a sinful man, O Lord" (Luke 5:8). Cyril of Jerusalem tells his catechumens, "Sin is . . . a fearful evil for him who clings to it, but easy of cure for him who by repentance puts it from him" (*Cat. Lect.*, 2, 1). Like Peter, we must openly admit our sinfulness—it is essential for true conversion (see Psalm 32:5). Repentance, which is open admission of sin, is the door we need to walk through in order to obtain freedom and new life in the Spirit. Jesus himself calls us saying, "I have not come to call the righteous, but sinners to repentance" (Luke 5:32). His call was repeated by the apostles after Pentecost (see Acts 2:38, 3:19, 5:31, 8:22, 11:18, 17:30, 20:21, 26:20).

Repentance means change—having a change of heart. The Greek word *metanoia*, meaning to turn the mind around, to change the direction of one's life, sums it up. To repent is to turn our back on sin and our hearts and minds towards God. When we are convicted by the Holy Spirit of our sinfulness and of the truth of the gospel, we must turn to God and express both sorrow for sin and a firm desire not to sin again. The latter is essential for true repentance. Sorrow for sin is our first response, but it should lead to a change of heart, mind and desire, to a decision to live a new life of virtue, keeping God's commands. John the Baptist means exactly that when he tells the Pharisees they must "bear fruits that befit repentance" (Luke 3:8), which are love of God and love of the brethren.

Concerning repentance, Paul distinguishes between godly grief and worldly grief. To the Corinthians he wrote, "Godly grief produces a repentance that leads to salvation and brings no regret, but worldly grief produces death" (2 Corinthians 7:10). Godly grief leads us to recognize our sinfulness before God and the harm done both to his majesty and to our brothers and sisters. Recognizing our sin, we desire to flee from such evil, to seek salvation in God's forgiveness and the power of his Spirit to change our lives. Paul says that such repentance produces the good fruit of eagerness, zeal, indignation and longing (2 Corinthians 7:11). Paul says, too, that such repentance brings no regret. When we manifest godly grief and true repentance, we do not return to our sin; we do not renege on our repentance.

Worldly grief, on the other hand, brings nothing but death. Seeing our sin, we experience only hurt pride, the devastating discovery that we are not perfect. We grieve not over the evil done, but over our bruised egos. Such grief is selfish and self-centered. It does not lead to true repentance but to excuses and deception as we stubbornly refuse to change, and seek instead to rationalize and hide our state before God and man. Such behavior shows no signs of the convicting and fruit-bearing work of the Holy Spirit.

To our fallen natures, the gospel summons to repentance is dreaded, unwelcome and repugnant. Yet the ability to repent and to seek forgiveness is itself a great gift from God, a true work of the Holy Spirit in our lives. If God had not given the gift of repentance, we would die in sin and guilt, and experience his wrath.

Paul tells the Romans, "Do you not know that God's kindness is meant to lead you to repentance? But by your hard and impenitent heart you are storing up wrath for yourself on the day of wrath when God's righteous judgment will be revealed" (Romans 2:4-5). The author of 2 Peter explains that Jesus has not returned in glory because he is "forbearing toward you, not wishing that you should perish, but that all should reach repentance" (3:9). God knows better than we the dire consequences of an unrepentant heart (see Revelation 2:23 ff., 9:20, 16:9, 11).

God's love for sinners, ultimately expressed in Jesus' incarnation and death on the cross, makes repentance possible (see Hosea 2:4-24). To repent is to take advantage of God's love, to appropriate the benefits of Jesus' cross, and to assent to the truth the Holy Spirit reveals.

Cyril of Jerusalem emphasizes the efficacy of repentance founded on God's love. He counsels his listeners not to despair in their sin, as if their sin were too great. "For it is a fearful thing not to believe in a hope of repentance" (*Cat. Lect.*, 2, 5). God's love, he says, will pardon all sin and he lists many people in the Old Testament God has forgiven, including Moses, David and Solomon. Jesus forgave Peter, who denied him. God is even willing to forgive those who crucified his Son. Therefore, Cyril concludes,

> Take heed lest without reason you mistrust the power of repentance. Would that you would know that power repentance has. Would that you would know the strong weapon of salvation, and learn what the force of confession is.

> *(ibid.,* 2, 15)

The great power of repentance lies in the Holy Spirit: he moves us to repent and he cleanses from sin. Repentance is truly the work of the Holy Spirit of God.

Christians need to repent every day for the sin in their lives. Nonetheless, the act of repentance that comes with conversion is special and important because the Holy Spirit then, for the first time, reveals our rebellious sinful nature and our own personal participation in sin; and we can then, in truth, acknowledge it and make a life-changing decision, by the power of the Spirit, to turn from sin and to turn to God. All other repentance flows from our initial decision to make a radical change in our lives.

The Power Of Confession

In theory, when we recognize sin, our immediate response should be repentance. In practice, however, we often struggle against it. Paul speaks from his own experience saying,

> For I do not do the good I want, but the evil I do not want is what I do. So I find it to be a law that when I want to do right, evil lies close at hand. For I delight in the law of God, in my inmost self, but I see in my members another law at war with the law of my mind and making me captive to the

> law of sin which dwells in my members. Wretched
> man that I am! Who will deliver me from this
> body of death? Thanks be to God through Jesus
> Christ our Lord!
>
> *(Romans 7:19, 21-25)*

Often, part of us wants to cling to sin. We hesitate to turn
our lives completely over to God. We struggle with the
truth God has revealed, refusing to use the power of the
Spirit that is offered to us to overcome sin.

St. Augustine is the classic example of a man struggling
with sin in the process of conversion. He had lived with a
mistress for many years, but as the truth of the gospel and
the light of the Spirit penetrated his mind, he was convicted of his sin. According to his biography, when God
showed him the truth, he would say, "'A minute', 'just a
minute', 'just a little time longer.' But there was no limit to
the minutes, and the 'little time longer' went a long way"
(*Conf.*, 8, 5). Augustine would pray, "'Make me chaste and
continent, but not yet.' I was afraid that you might hear
me too soon and cure me too soon from the disease of a
lust which I preferred to be satisfied rather than extinguish-
ed" (*ibid.*, 8, 7). He concluded that he is a true son of Adam.

> As to me, when I was deliberating about entering
> the service of the Lord my God, and had long
> intended to do so, it was I who willed it, and it
> was I who was unwilling. It was the same 'I'
> throughout. But neither my will nor my unwil-
> lingness was whole and entire. So I fought with
> myself and was torn apart.
>
> *(Conf., 8, 10)*

Augustine's torn will was finally healed when God spoke
to him in scripture (see Romans 13:13-14). He immediately

realized it was only with the Spirit's help that he could give his life to Christ and live as a committed Christian. His struggle had ended.

Augustine's struggle, leading to final submission to God, is a paradigm of conversion. Each of us struggles to give up sin. Each of us must also call on the Holy Spirit, asking him to enable our wills to desire and grasp the salvation of Jesus Christ. Mature fellow Christians—priests, teachers and parents—can be instruments of the Holy Spirit in helping us reject sin and turn to Christ. They can help us see our sin more clearly, as well as encourage us to repent and seek the goodness of the Lord. James exhorts us to remember that "whoever brings back a sinner from the error of his way will save his soul from death and will cover a multitude of sins" (James 5:20).

One of the signs that genuine conversion is actually taking place is our willingness to bring our sin into the light. In John's Gospel, Jesus says that "everyone who does evil hates the light, and does not come to the light, lest his deeds should be exposed" (John 3:20). Exposing sin to the light of Christ is a sure way of letting go of sin and evil, and entering into the light of Christ' salvation. It frees sinners—us—from the bondage of guilt and the condemnation of Satan.

This is why Cyril so strongly encouraged his catechumens to be honest with themselves before God and to confess their sin. "The present is the season of confession: confess what you have done in word or in deed, by night and by day; confess in an acceptable time and in the day of salvation receive the heavenly treasure" (*Cat. Lect.*, 1, 5). For Cyril sin "candidly confessed" receives a "most speedy cure" (ibid., 2, 11). So powerful is the confession of sin that he concludes, "Turn and bewail yourself, shut your door, and pray to be forgiven, pray that He may remove from you the burning flames. For confession has power to quench even fire, power to tame even lions" (*ibid.*, 2, 15).

Catholics normally associate confession of sin with the sacrament of reconciliation. This sacrament is especially beneficial for non-practicing Catholics coming to a new and full conversion to Christ. The sacrament of reconciliation can be an important turning point in our lives, if we have truly heard the gospel preached and are properly prepared. Within this sacrament, probably for the first time, we can maturely repent of our sinful state and for the many sins of our past. We can honestly admit we are sinners in need of forgiveness and redemption, and rightly take full responsibility for our sinful condition without making excuses. Then, for the first time, we will know God's forgiveness. Our confession allows God to lift the burden of guilt and cleanse our consciences in the blood of Christ who died for our sins (see Hebrews 9:14).

Practicing Catholics who recognize the need for deeper conversion can obtain similar benefits. In the past, the church has encouraged what was called "general confession" at important times during our lives: marriage, religious profession, parish missions. This practice can help us, if we are properly prepared, to realize in a new and deeper way the sin in our lives. It allows us to see more clearly our true need for salvation and a life committed to Jesus. It can also free us from the burden of guilt lingering from the past and heal our hearts and minds of sin's effects. The sacrament of reconciliation is not magic, but it can be an important moment in the process of conversion and a deeper life of faith. The Holy Spirit can work through it in a powerful way.

The sacrament of reconciliation should not, however, be the only place where we bring our sin to light. Husbands and wives should not be afraid to let one another know their sins and failings. Done prudently, such sharing can build up their relationship. It brings honesty, openness and forthrightness. It dispels resentments, anger and deceitfulness. Spouses can help each other overcome patterns of sin and encourage and pray for one another. Parents should also foster in their children an attitude of openness and honesty about sin. Children should be encouraged to admit their temptations, struggles and failings. Parents can foster this openness by learning how to ask the right kind of questions and by talking discriminately about weaknesses in their own lives. Trying to hide our sins in a family setting is an impossible task that breeds nothing but pride and defensiveness. Open admission of our sinful condition allows the Holy Spirit to heal the effects of sin in our families, enabling each member to appropriate the saving power of Christ. Openness also brings forth the Spirit's fruits of joy, peace and love within the family (see Galatians 5:22).

Deliverance

In the new rite of catechumens, the priest prays for deliverance of the catechumens saying, "Breathe your Spirit, Lord, and drive out the spirits of evil: command them to depart, for your kingdom is drawing near." Later the priest prays,

All-powerful and ever-living God, through your only Son you promised us the Holy Spirit. We pray for our brothers and sisters who present themselves as catechumens. Keep far from them every evil spirit and all falsehood and sin, that they may become temples of your Holy Spirit. Confirm with your power what we speak in faith, that our words may not be empty, but

spoken in the strength and grace of your Son
who freed the world from evil.

Exorcism has also been a part of coming to know Christ.
In the early church, exorcism and deliverance were con-
sidered necessary elements in conversion: converts were
leaving the kingdom of Satan and entering the kingdom of
God, and the power and hold of Satan had to be broken.
Cyril does not hesitate to say that purity of life cannot be
attained without exorcism. "Let your feet hasten to the
catechizings; receive with earnestness the exorcism: whether you be breathed upon or exorcised, the act is to your
salvation" (*Procat.*, 9). St. Ignatius of Loyola also expresses
the importance of exorcism, describing conversion as the
move from living under the standard of Satan to living
under the standard of Jesus Christ. We renounce the three
temptations of Satan, riches, honor and pride, and choose
instead "the supreme and true Leader, who is Christ our
Lord" (*Spiritual Exercises,* second week, day four).

For this reason, the church has also always insisted on
the need for a special alertness to his wiles during the time
of conversion. He will try to confuse us about the truth of
the gospel. He will try to get us to compromise on the
reality of our sin, and will attempt to water down the
truth of salvation. He will tempt us with fear of what we
will lose in coming to faith in Jesus, and attempt to harden
our hearts. He will be out to sow chaos in our lives. Cyril
warns the catechumens that while they are coming into
the glory of God, "there is a serpent by the wayside
watching those who pass by: beware lest he bite you with
unbelief. He sees so many receiving salvation, and is
seeking whom he may devour" (*Procat.*, 16).

Prayers for exorcism are part of the official prayer of the
church for catechumens and those who are to be baptized.

Therefore, in the strict sense, prayers of exorcism should not be performed haphazardly or by unqualified persons. Exorcism is not something to toy with on your own. Since Satan can be active in a variety of ways and influence us in many situations, however, we should not be afraid to pray that we and others be delivered from the wiles and snares of Satan. All of us, priests and laity alike, pray for this every time we pray the words Jesus gave us in the Our Father, "deliver us from evil. . ."

Many situations call for alertness to Satan's influence, and prayers for deliverance are appropriate. When we, whether priests, religious, married or single people, find in ourselves or others patterns of uncontrolled sin, we should request and encourage prayer for deliverance from Satan's influence or hold. Uncontrolled anger, resentment, jealousy, lust, lying, stealing, excessive drinking, and fears are common manifestations of Satan's grip. We should not be shocked or fearful because Satan does influence us. He is out to destroy lives, and our broken natures make us easy prey for his schemes and lies. Peter tells his readers, "Be sober, be watchful. Your adversary the devil prowls around like a roaring lion, seeking someone to devour. Resist him, firm in your faith. . . ."(1 Peter 5:8-9).

On the cross, Jesus conquered Satan and the bondage of sin (see Romans 6-8). Just as the Spirit empowered Jesus to foil the tempter, so now Christians who possess the power of the Spirit can ward off Satan's attacks. Paul tells the Christians of Ephesus that with "the shield of faith" and "the sword of the Spirit" they can "quench all the flaming darts of the evil one" (Ephesians 6:16-17).

Examination of Conscience

Daily examination of conscience is one of the cornerstones of our faith, along with prayer and the scriptures. It is the only way we can continually be alert to our sin, become clear about our state before God and allow the Holy Spirit to bring us to repentance and the joy of God's loving forgiveness. All of the saints and the entire spiritual tradition of the Church have emphasized our need for regular examination of conscience and its many benefits. It is essential for ongoing conversion and growth in holiness and, moreover, allows the Spirit to foster new attitudes and disclose new responsibilities to care for others.

The best time for an examination of conscience for adults is usually at the beginning of daily prayer time. Forgiven and released from the burden of sin, we can experience the return of clarity and freedom, and then praise and worship the Trinity with enthusiasm and conviction.

How should we examine our consciences daily? To start with, spend a short time; five minutes, at most, should be adequate. Make a list of God's commands and the particular responsibilities we have as priests, religious, single people, or parents, and measure our thoughts and actions against it. Many scripture passages are particularly helpful. For example, the Ten Commandments are the foundation of any examination of conscience. They are listed in Exodus 20:2-17 and Deuteronomy 5:6-21. Paul's letter contains some very good passages for examining our lives, including the one from Galatians quoted at the beginning of this chapter, Ephesians 4:17-32, 15-21 and Colossians 3:5-17. Jesus' Sermon on the Mount recorded in Matthew 5-7 also makes an excellent examinination of conscience. Read these passages and write down on a card points that pertain specifically to you. Keep this card with you and look at it as your examine your conscience.

Athletes, television personalities, journalists, business-men and women and others who strive for excellence constantly evaluate their performance and professionalism. They desire to be the best and to develop their talents and competence. As Christians, we should expect and desire nothing less in our spiritual lives. Examining our consciences is a means of quality control for our Christian lives. Are we keeping God's commands? Are we living up to God's standard? Are we fulfilling our responsibilities? Where do we need to change? What can we do better as spouses or parents? We will never know, and the Holy Spirit will never be able to tell us and help us, if we do not examine our lives daily. Examination of conscience leads to continual conversion and growth. As we faithfully examine our lives, God's love and Jesus' salvation will more deeply penetrate our hearts and minds.

We have examined how the Holy Spirit convicts us of sin, helps us overcome struggles and leads us to mature repentance. Stop now, before you move to the next chapter. Ask the Spirit to reveal to you where you have sin you haven't repented for.

- Where are you struggling?
- Are there people, your spouse or children perhaps, whom you have not forgiven or toward whom you have resentments?
- What responsibilities have you not fulfilled?
- Most of all, do you see that you are a son or daughter of Adam and Eve—fallen, broken, sinful?
- Do you recognize at the core of your being there is a rebelliousness against God that is displayed in sinful actions?
- Do you see your absolute need for salvation in Jesus Christ?

Chapter Six

Faith In The
Lord Jesus Christ

T
HE HOLY SPIRIT BRINGS FAITH TO LIFE IN OUR
hearts and, through the faith born in us, comes
to dwell within us. We must only be receptive,
for faith is a free gift that must be accepted in
gratitude. The Holy Spirit can then lead us all—non-
believer, maturing child, nominal Christian—opening our
ears to hear the truth of the gospel, convicting us of sin
and bringing us to repentance. The work of the Spirit
culminates when we come to mature faith, which enables
the Spirit to abide within our hearts and minds. The
Fathers of Vatican II summarize clearly this intimate
relationship between faith and the Holy Spirit.

> The obedience of faith (Romans 16:26; cf. Romans
> 1:5; 2 Corinthians 10:5-6) must be given to God
> as he reveals himself. By faith man freely com-
> mits his entire self to God, making "the full sub-
> mission of his intellect and will to God who
> reveals," and willingly assenting to the Revela-
> tion given by him. Before this faith can be exer-
> cised, man must have the grace of God to move
> and assist him; he must have the interior helps of

the Holy Spirit, who moves the heart and converts it to God, who opens the eyes of the mind
and "makes it easy for all to accept and believe
the truth." The same Holy Spirit constantly per-
fects faith by his gifts, as that Revelation may be
more and more profoundly understood.

(D.V., 5)

We want to examine here the nature and effects of
faith, and how we can foster it in our lives and the lives of
others. As you read on, ask the Holy Spirit to help you
compare your faith and the faith of the members of your
families with the faith described in scripture. The Spirit
wants you to be clear about it so he can give you the fullness of faith needed to enjoy the fullness of God's glory.

Faith in the Old Testament

The Old Testament word for faith is derived from the
Hebrew word *aman*, which bears the sense of being solid or
firm and, therefore, true. We hold something to be true
when it has these qualities, and God is the ultimate source
of dependability, security and firmness. He is trustworthy,
hence we can depend on him for the truth. Our trust is
founded upon his fidelity (see Psalms 36:5-6, 40:11, 7:22).

Abraham is a good example of the Old Testament
understanding of faith. In fact, he has come to be known
as "The Father of Faith" precisely because he is the epi-
tome of what it means to have faith and trust in God. "It is
men of faith who are the sons of Abraham" (Galatians
3:7).

Abraham, who was named Abram before God called
him, lived in Ur of the Chaldeans in Mesopotamia. God
came to him and said,

> Go from your country and your kindred and
> your father's house to the land that I will show
> you. And I will bless you, and make your name
> great, so that you will be a blessing. I will bless
> those who bless you, and him who curses you I
> will curse; and by you all the families of the earth
> shall bless themselves.
>
> *(Genesis 12:1-3)*

Abram trusted God's word and, although he was aged, left
his homeland for a place unknown.

God brought Abram to the promised land and blessed
him. Though Abram did not yet have any legitimate children, God was faithful to him promising, "'Look toward
heaven, and number the stars, if you are able to number
them.' Then he said to him, 'So shall your descendants be'"
(Genesis 15:5). Abram "believed the Lord; and he reckoned
it to him as righteousness" (Genesis 15:6). Despite his old
age and his wife's barrenness, Abram held as truth God's
promise that he would have a son. He believed and
counted God's word a fact, therefore God acknowledged
that Abram was holy, righteous and just before him. God
made a covenant with Abram, changing his name to
Abraham "for I have made you the father of a multitude of
nations" (Genesis 17:5). Even though Abraham's wife,
Sarah, laughed at the thought of bearing a child, she conceived and bore a son, Isaac (see Genesis 18:12, 21:1-3) just
as God had promised.

God's faithfulness and promise that Abraham would be
a father of a great nation rested on Isaac. Then God put
Abraham to a test, asking him to sacrifice Isaac. To all
appearances, God was becoming unfaithful, going back on
his word, reneging on the covenant. Abraham prepared to
do as God commanded, however, for his faith was stronger

than appearance and human reasoning. God stopped him at the last moment saying, "Do not lay your hand on the lad or do anything to him; for now I know that you fear God, seeing you have not withheld your son, your only son, from me" (Genesis 22:12).

From the moment God intervened in his life, Abraham believed God's word and trusted in his faithfulness. He was obedient to God's every word and loyal to him in the face of apparent contradiction because he was confident of God's fidelity. He staked his life (and that of his nation) on God and God's promises to him, and he was not disappointed. St. Paul extols Abraham's faith,

> In hope he believed against hope, that he should become the father of many nations. . . . He did not weaken in faith when he considered his own body, which was as good as dead . . . No distrust made him waver concerning the promise of God, but he grew strong in his faith as he gave glory to God, fully convinced that God was able to do what he had promised.
>
> *(Romans 4:18-21)*

Abraham was a man of faith and is truly "the father of us all" (Romans 4:16). For other Old Testament examples of faith, see Hebrews 11 and the corresponding references in the Old Testament.

In the Old Testament, faith is founded on the faithfulness of God, whose fidelity is seen specifically in the context of the covenant and covenant-virtue, *hesed*, and God's loving kindness towards his people. Only because the Israelites recognized and acknowledged God's love and commitment to them were they able to believe in him and keep his commandments. Faith is their stance before God, they are postured in trust, confidence and security, ready to do his will.

Faith brings knowledge of God. In the Old Testament, true knowledge of God is not intellectual or abstract, but personal and experiential. In faith, the people came to know and experience Yahweh himself (see Psalm 34; Deuteronomy 4:32-40). Their knowledge of God comes from his action in their lives. A person of faith, then is not someone who merely knows about God, but someone who knows God himself, in a personal way. Faith establishes a living relationship with God.

The personal knowledge of God that comes by faith is illustrated in the Book of Job. While not historical in nature, it does proclaim in story form important truths about God's relationship to man. Job, angered by his plight, complains bitterly to God that he has been treated unjustly. God appears to him and confronts him with the disparity between the almighty wisdom and knowledge of God and Job's own meager understanding. "I will question, and you declare to me. . . . Have you an arm like God, and . . . a voice like his?" (Job 40:9). Humbled, Job professes that he has arrogantly spoken of things he does not understand. Job concludes, "I have heard of thee by the hearing of the ear, but now my eyes see thee; therefore I despise myself, and repent in dust and ashes" (Job 42:5-6).

Job had heard of God many times. He knew all about him. Intellectually, he had grasped that God is all powerful and almighty, but experiencing God personally added a life-changing dimension to Job's relationship to God. After that experience, he not only knew about God, he actually knew God himself. Job was forced to recognize his own sinful, humble position and the true awesome glory of God. This work of faith in Job's life brought him into personal contact with none other than the living God!

Faith in the New Testament

The Old Testament understanding of faith is the foundation for the New Testament understanding. The Greek words, *pistis* (faith) and *pisteuein* (to believe), frequently used in original New Testament manuscripts, connote trust, confidence in, acceptance as true. "Faith is the assurance of things hoped for, the conviction of things not seen" (Hebrews 11:1). In the New Testament, faith is centered on Jesus Christ.

For St. Paul, faith in Jesus Christ justifies us before God. We are justified not "by works of the law but through faith in Jesus Christ" (Galatians 2:16; see 3:24, 5:1, 6:12-15). Justification is a gift from God, won by Jesus on the cross and freely given to all who believe (see Romans 5-8).

> If you confess with your lips that Jesus is Lord and believe in your heart that God raised him from the dead, you will be saved. For man believes with his heart and so is justified, and he confesses with his lips and so is saved.
>
> *(Romans 10:9-10)*

Everyone of us must grasp this important truth. We tend to believe that somehow we can or must make ourselves "right" with God. We imagine that by doing good deeds, helping people and being kind, or by our pleasing and upright personalities we can stand justified before God. We think our good deeds will outweigh our bad deeds, therefore God will judge us "holy" and allow us to enter heaven. Paul tells Titus, however, that

> When the goodness and loving kindness of God our Savior appeared, he saved us, not because of deeds done by us in righteousness, but in virtue

> of his own mercy, by the washing of regenera-
> tion and renewal in the Holy Spirit.
>
> (*Titus 3:4-5*)

Our natural attitude is not right. Because of our sin, we can never, on our own, make ourselves right with God. Our good deeds will never outweigh our bad deeds, and can never save us. God's salvation is an entirely free gift we receive when we come to faith in Jesus Christ. Many people falsely presume that they are not so "bad" or that they are actually "good" and therefore God will reward them. This is not true. We can never obtain salvation by "proving" our worthiness. God's salvation comes only through Jesus Christ, and we receive it through faith in him.

This is not to say that "works" avail nothing; since we have been justified by faith, we have a responsibility to live a life worthy of our calling (see Ephesians 4:1). "Faith apart from works is barren" (James 2:20). In fact, God expects and demands that we cooperate with his grace, by keeping his commands and performing the works of charity he calls us to do. In this way, we advance our salvation. Our cooperation, however, is due solely to the Holy Spirit within us, who enables us to do what God demands.

St. Paul teaches that we are justified by faith, and that we also receive justification through the Holy Spirit who dwells within us. Paul rhetorically asks the Galatians, "Did you receive the Spirit by works of the law, or by hearing with faith?" (Galatians 3:2). As the Holy Spirit leads us to faith, he springs to life within us, transforming us from slaves of sin to righteous ones before God. The Letter to the Ephesians says,

> In him [Christ] you also, who have heard the
> word of truth, the gospel of your salvation, and

have believed in him, were sealed with the promised Holy Spirit, which is the guarantee of our
inheritance until we acquire possession of it to
the praise of his glory.

(Ephesians 1:13-14)

Because the Spirit comes to life within us, we possess an
entirely new relationship with God. Through the Spirit,
Jesus recreates us as true sons or daughters of the Father.
In prayer, Jesus called his Father, "Abba" (see Mark 14:36),
the affectionate, intimate and familial Hebrew word for
father, like our English word "dad." (Children in Israel still
use this word today.) Jesus could speak intimately to God
because he is the eternal and natural Son of the Father
who, with the Father, possesses the Holy Spirit. Only
Christians possess the indwelling Spirit, therefore only
they can in truth address God as fully adopted children.
"Because you are sons, God has sent the Spirit of his Son
into our hearts, crying 'Abba! Father!' So through God you
are no longer a slave but a son, and if a son then an heir"
(Galatians 4:6-7; see Romans 8:15-16). We share this same
Spirit, which the Son had by nature, making us true children of God.

This is not an intolerant or narrow belief, but a proclamation of God's love and mercy. The Father sent his Son
into the world precisely so that all people, of all nations,
could become his true children through faith and the Holy
Spirit. Our justification through faith and the Holy Spirit
cannot be over-emphasized. We can presume that because
God created us, each one of us is automatically a child of
God and, in one sense, this is true. God is the father of all
because he is responsible for creation and the life of each
individual. Because of sin, however, we do not naturally
have an intimate and personal relationship with God as
our Father. Lack of a personal relationship with God is not

72

a judgment against anyone, but rather a call to all people to become children of the eternal Father through faith in his Son, Jesus. The marvelous gift of belonging to the Father and sharing in the life and love of his Spirit must be esteemed and treasured in our families and among our friends. It will attract others and help them value our great Christian privilege.

Knowing Christ

We might think Jesus' contemporaries had an advantage over us because they walked and talked with him on earth. This is not true. Because Jesus is risen in glory and can send forth his Spirit into our hearts, we are able to know Jesus better and relate to him more personally and intimately than the people who walked the streets of Jerusalem with him. Jesus himself said that it is better that he go (see John 16:7). After Pentecost, the apostles never looked back nostalgically. They knew Jesus was in their midst in a way far superior to that by which they had seen him on earth, for he was with them through faith and the Holy Spirit. He lived within them (see John 14:23) and he can live within us in the same way.

St. Paul tells us that we live new lives in Christ because the Holy Spirit dwells within us (see Galatians 3:22; Romans 3:22, 28; Philippians 3:9; Ephesians 3:12). Living in Christ is the basis of our personal and spiritual knowledge of Jesus, who in the Holy Spirit reveals himself interiorly to us as the eternal Son of the Father. Jesus is no longer just an historical figure, but a living person with whom we can intimately relate. Paul tells the Colossians that they "live in him, rooted and built up in him and established in the faith" (Colossians 2:6). Paul is so confident of this personal knowledge of Christ that he prays we might be strengthened in the Spirit and that

> Christ may dwell in your hearts through faith;
> that you, being rooted and grounded in love, may
> have power to comprehend with all the saints
> what is the breadth and length and height and
> depth, and to know the love of Christ which sur-
> passes knowledge, that you may be filled with all
> the fullness of God.
>
> *(Ephesians 3:17-19)*

For Paul, and for each of us, everything is worthless "because of the surpassing worth of knowing Christ Jesus my Lord" (Philippians 3:8).

We must hold in reverence and awe the reality of know-ing Christ and the Father's love for us. No greater honor or privilege has been conferred upon us than to know Jesus and his salvation. Conscious of this great privilege, we should incite others to desire to know Jesus, and assure them that such personal knowledge is not mysterious or strange, but the very heart and center of Christian life.

St. John's understanding of faith is basically the same as St. Paul's, and he wrote his gospel precisely so "that you may believe that Jesus is the Christ, the Son of God and that believing you may have life in his name" (John 20:31). John emphasizes that to believe in Jesus is to become a child of God and possess eternal life (see John 1:12, 3:15, 5:24), and records Jesus often stating that faith in him is essential. "This is the work of God, that you believe in him whom he has sent" (John 6:29, see also John 12:36).

Is It Reasonable to Believe?

We often hear that it is unreasonable to believe. Faith is an irrational act. The reasonable person only holds to be true only what can be reasonably grasped and understood. The truths of faith cannot be proved empirically, therefore they should not be believed. It is impossible to do a laboratory test to determine if Jesus is God, nor can Jesus' resurrected body be examined. Even children might question how they are to believe something they cannot see or fully understand, and obviously we cannot fully understand how God is three Persons and yet only one God, or how the eternal Son is both God and man.

How are we to answer the difficulties and objections raised above? Do we just say, "It's a mystery"? Do we tell our children, "Don't ask questions, just believe"? Such pat answers won't satisfy anyone very long. We must have faith, which St. Augustine calls "thinking with assent" (*De Praedest. Sant.*, 2, 5). Thinking with the eyes of faith will help us understand what we believe.

The primary point to remember is that the whole process of conversion and coming to faith is a work of the Holy Spirit in our hearts and minds. The Spirit's light enables us to see the reasonableness of faith and gives our minds a grasp of what we must believe. St. Cyril of Jerusalem states that "Faith is an eye that enlightens every conscience, and imparts understanding" (*1 Cat. Lect.*, 5, 4). For example, the Holy Spirit convicts us of sin and enlightens our minds to understand that we have fallen and that our participation in that fall is not unreasonable but wholly true. The Spirit also helps us grasp that Jesus, the Incarnate Son of God, has saved mankind from sin and death. When we hear the gospel preached, the Holy Spirit gives us both an understanding of the mysteries of faith and the ensuing conviction to believe they are true realities in which we can participate.

St. Augustine was aware of the Holy Spirit's work in our minds, bringing us to faith when he wrote,

> For although no one can believe in God unless he
> understands something, nonetheless the faith by

which he believes heals him, so that he may
understand more fully. For there are some things
which we believe only if we understand and
other things which we understand only if we
believe.   (*In Ps.*, 118)

Through the work of the Spirit, we come to the conviction
and understanding of the mysteries of faith. St. Anselm
echoed the words of Augustine when he said, "I do not
seek to understand in order to believe; but I believe in
order to understand" (*Pros.*, 1). Aided by the power of the
Spirit, we seek in faith to understand what God has
revealed in word and action. Faith enables us to know and
experience the revelation of God, and "understanding is
the reward of faith" (St. Augustine, *In Joh.*, 29, 6).

We should remember the work of the Spirit when ques-
tioning or examining our faith. We need to ask questions
that will allow him to penetrate our hearts and minds,
because conversion occurs as God touches and changes
our lives. Questions about how the all-good, all-powerful
God can allow horrendous evil in the world, or blatantly
corrupt Popes to head his church, might be valid and
deserve answers, but they are not the central issue. In fact,
they are side issues that can deflect what God wants to do
in our lives. We must confront the true issue: does God
exist? Will we allow him to manifest his existence and
reveal his infinite love to us? Is Jesus Lord? Will we recognize our need to be reconciled to God through faith in
Jesus Christ? Will we ask Jesus to reveal the truth that he
died for our sins and rose to give us new life? These are
the important questions. We must face them and act upon
them. The side issues tend to cloud what is at stake—our
lives. We need to focus on the true questions and not get
sidetracked on less crucial and distracting matters.

What should we do then, when we ourselves sincerely say, "I can't believe Jesus is God" or "I don't see how I am a sinner" or "I don't understand how God can be a Trinity"? First, we must determine whether we understand the truths of faith. If we are not sure we do, we should read and study the scriptures or speak to a mature Christian who can answer our questions clearly. (Rereading chapter two of this book might help, for it states clearly basic truths of our faith.) If we still find it difficult to assent to the truths, the only effective action we can take is to seek enlightenment and conviction from the Holy Spirit. Only the Spirit can give us understanding of the reality of Jesus and the evil of sin. Only he can give us faith. We can be sure that if we humbly and sincerely ask the Spirit for understanding, he will act in power. It is impossible for such a prayer to go unheeded—Jesus died so that this prayer might be answered! Jesus reigns now in glory, interceding for us before the throne of God the Father. He desires with all his heart to pour his Spirit into our hearts. If we ask for faith and understanding, he will give them to us. We will become men and women of faith.

Can We Be Certain?

If we possess Christian faith, we hold our beliefs as absolutely true. Our certitude comes, not from convincing logical arguments, although they might play a legitimate role, but from the convicting power of the Holy Spirit. Compare this attitude with contemporary use of the words "faith" and "belief." In ordinary speech, faith and belief are synonymous with opinion and probability. A person who believes the hometown football team is the best is expressing an opinion. Someone who believes investing in the stock market is the best way to ensure financial security and growth is expressing a probability.

They might actually be true, but other reasonable options could also be correct. A rival football team might defeat the hometown team. The stock market could collapse or money market bonds could soar. The reasonable person realizes and acknowledges such possibilities.

Faith and belief in Christian truths are far different. Faith in Jesus Christ is not just personal opinion or reasoned probability. It is not one of many options, even if it does seem to be the best one. By the light of the Holy Spirit, we can be absolutely sure that what God has revealed through Christ Jesus is true beyond any doubt. All opposed religious claims are not true. Others may say that what we hold in faith is an opinion, but we are sure that what we believe is irrevocably true.

The Letter to the Hebrews clearly expresses this understanding of Christian faith. "Now faith is the assurance of things hoped for, the conviction of things not seen" (Hebrews 11:1). We can be interiorly sure and confident that what we believe will actually come about. Our hope for salvation, resurrection of the body and eternal life is beyond question. We can be convicted of the truths of the gospel even though we do not see them with our physical eyes, or grasp them fully with our intellects. We can know through faith that God is a Trinity of persons, that Jesus is God and man, that he now reigns in glory before the throne of the Father. Faith born of the Holy Spirit can dispel any skepticism, lingering doubt or hesitancy to believe.

We do not need to be apologetic about the certitude of our faith. It is a gift of the Holy Spirit. We run the risk of becoming "nominal" Christians when we lose our certitude in the midst of contemporary religious philosophies. Every day we hear statements like, "With everyone saying something different, who can say who is right?" "How do we know that Zen Buddhism isn't true or that transcendental meditation isn't best for some people?" "Religion is a personal thing. What's best and true for one person might not be right for someone else." Even children can be influenced by this religious relativity, since it permeates their peer relationships and the schools they attend. In the face of such cultural pressure, we need to pray constantly for the assurance and clarity, asking the Holy Spirit for the convicting power of faith. As long as we keep the basic truths of the gospel in our minds clearly and unambiguously, we will not falter or become confused. We must constantly build up our faith by our own unwavering certainty, relying on the light and strength of the Holy Spirit. As we live the Christian life in the Spirit, our own experiences will prove the truth of the gospel to us and others. Paul exhorts Timothy and all of us saying,

> Follow the pattern of the sound words which you have heard from me, in the faith and love which are in Christ Jesus; guard the truth that has been entrusted to you by the Holy Spirit who dwells within us.
>
> (2 Timothy 1:13-14)

As we end this chapter on faith, ask the Holy Spirit to produce in you a confidence and certitude about the Christian truths. God loves us. The very Son of God became man. He died for us even though we are sinners. He rose from the dead and reigns in glory. The Holy Spirit is now being poured out on all the world. We are called to eternal life as sons and daughters of the all-holy God.

"Father, Son and Holy Spirit, we believe in you. We give our lives to you. We commit our entire being to you. Justify us in faith. Pour forth the Holy Spirit upon us. Forgive us for our sin. Break all sinful desires and actions. Take from us all uncertainty and confusion. Give us clarity, truth and conviction of heart and mind. To you alone, Father, Son and Holy Spirit, be all glory and honor. May all peoples, nations and races praise you for ever."

Part III
The Sacraments Of Initiation

THE CHURCH HAS ALWAYS VIEWED BAPTISM, CON-firmation and the eucharist as sacraments of initiation into the full Christian life. In the process of adult conversion, they are the culmination and entrance into mature life in the Spirit and full participation in the worship and life of Christ's body, the church. The Fathers of Vatican II describe the progression into the Christian life this way:

> Incorporated into the Church by Baptism, the faithful are appointed by their baptismal character to Christian religious worship; reborn as sons of God, they must profess before men the faith they have received from God through the Church. By the sacrament of Confirmation they are more perfectly bound to the Church and are endowed with the special strength of the Holy Spirit. Hence they are, as true witnesses of Christ, more strictly obliged to spread the faith by word and deed. Taking part in the eucharistic sacrifice, the source and summit of the Christian life, they offer the divine victim to God and themselves along with it.
>
> (L.G., 11)

This section of the book examines the sacraments' relation to conversion and the work of the Holy Spirit in our lives. As you read, ask the Spirit to help you see how truly important these sacraments are.

Chapter Seven

Baptism
And Confirmation

MOST OF US WERE BAPTIZED AS INFANTS. AS WE read this chapter, we might think, "I've been baptized, so all this has already happened to me," or, "I learned about baptism and confirmation in school when I was young. I already know all of this." In one sense, this might be true. We have been baptized. Through the power of the Holy Spirit, the Lord Jesus has done a wonderful work in us. The seed of faith has been planted. It would be a mistake, however, to approach this chapter as if being baptized and confirmed were the end of the story, period. Examine baptism, for example, from the perspective of what has been said in the previous chapters, which describe what is at the heart of that sacrament. Each of us has been baptized, but we must also lay hold of the reality of baptism as we mature, and take responsibility for its grace. We must learn to live the gospel, repent of sin and acknowledge in firm faith that Jesus is truly our Lord and Messiah. Unless we do, our baptism counts for nothing and does not bear the fruit which Christ intended it to. We must see it, not as an isolated liturgical rite, but as an essential aspect of the whole conversion process.

The sacraments of marriage and ordination are analagous to baptism. When two people get married, the Lord binds them together for life, and the Holy Spirit pours out a special grace. That, however, is just the beginning. The couple must take responsibility for the grace of marriage. They must live it out. If they do not, the sacrament of marriage will be of little value to them and, in time, they could easily separate and get a divorce. The same is true of a priest. Ordination itself does not guarantee that a man will be a holy, dedicated and responsible priest. He must live out his priesthood daily by the Holy Spirit's power.

In the same way, being baptized is not a guarantee that we are Christians. Though Jesus does act and the Spirit does come to dwell in us, we must take up the new life within us. We ourselves must live the gospel, or else the grace of baptism will have little effect. We can easily become Christians in name only, though this is obviously not what God desires. We are baptized so that the Holy Spirit can operate within us. We are called in faith to live, work and act responsibly in union with that Spirit.

We emphasize this point because so often today the lives of the baptized bear little resemblance to the Christian life. This undermines the dignity of the sacrament, causing some people to question the validity or efficacy of baptism. The problem, however, does not lie with the sacrament. Jesus does baptize. The Spirit is poured out. The problem is that many baptized persons have never taken responsibility for their baptism. They have never come to true and full conversion, thus the grace of baptism lies dormant and unused, and it can even die.

With this in mind, examine the sacraments of baptism and confirmation. You will see they are closely related to each other. As you read this chapter, look at the relationship between faith and baptism, the effect baptism has in our lives and the work of the Spirit, whom we receive at confirmation, in changing and equipping us to be mature witnesses of the gospel.

Baptism

From the beginning, the Church has viewed baptism as the climax of the conversion process. After hearing Peter's Pentecost sermon, the listeners were "cut to the heart" and asked Peter and the apostles, "Brethren, what shall we do?" Peter's response was, "Repent and be baptised every one of you in the name of Jesus Christ for the forgiveness of yours sins; and you shall receive the gift of the Holy Spirit"(Acts 2:37-38; see Acts 19:5).

There is an intrinsic relationship between faith and baptism. In adult conversion, faith normally leads to baptism, which is the certification of faith and the power to live it out. In baptism, the Spirit brings faith to life in our hearts and minds, setting his seal—himself—upon us, making us bona fide "believers" and commissioning us to live Christian lives. St. Basil says of the relationship between faith and baptism,

> Faith and baptism are two kindred and inseparable ways of salvation; faith is perfected by baptism; baptism is established by faith . . . as we believe in Father, Son and Holy Spirit, so we are baptised into the name of Father, Son and Holy Spirit. Confession leads the way and brings us to salvation; baptism follows, setting the seal on our assent.
>
> (De Spir. Sanct., 28)

The relationship between faith and baptism is evident in the rite of baptism, which historically has been preceded by a profession of faith. Today this profession takes the form of questions. The priest asks, "Do you reject Satan?" "Do you believe in God, the Father almighty, creator of heaven and earth?" The response to these and similar questions is, "I do." The priest concludes by proclaiming: "This is our faith. This is the faith of the Church. We are proud to profess it, in Christ Jesus our Lord" (*Rite of Baptism*).

Even for infants, faith and baptism cannot be separated. Here parents, godparents and the living Christian community supply faith for the child in the name of the church. To realize the fruit of baptism, the child must come to mature faith in adult life, for without faith, baptism and its effects will lie dormant. St. Augustine is very clear on this point:

> So in baptized infants the sacrament of regeneration comes first; and if they hold fast to Christian piety, conversion in the heart will follow, following as the sacramental sign of it in the body. This all shows that the sacrament of baptism is one thing, the conversion of the heart is another; but the salvation of man is effected by these two.
>
> (*De Bapt.*, 4, 31-32)

Augustine recognized the need for the conversion of children within Christian families. While no one promoted infant baptism more than Augustine, he knew that alone it is not enough, nor is it magic. Children do not automatically grow up to be Christians merely because they are baptized. They must hear the gospel and come to repentance and faith.

Augustine also grasped the problem of non-practicing "Christians" who have been baptized but in whom the Spirit has not worked conversion. The grace of baptism has not been brought to life in them through faith.

> We all know that if one baptized in infancy does
> not believe when he comes to years of discretion,
> and does not keep from himself lawless desires,
> then he will have no profit from the gift he
> received as a baby.
>
> (De Pecc. Merit., 1, 25)

Yet if personal faith is so essential, why baptize infants?
Why not wait until they are grown and can make an act of
faith on their own behalf?

We baptize infants for two reasons: to snatch them
from the grasp of Satan and to incorporate them into the
body of Christ. Born with original sin, babies do not
belong to the kingdom of God until they receive the Holy
Spirit, who frees them from the kingdom of darkness.
They are lovable and attractive, but nonetheless under the
domain of Satan. Christian parents must realize the truth
of their children's situation, and take the authority God
has invested them with to secure, through baptism, the
protection and love of God the Father for their children.
For this reason, the rite of baptism includes a beautiful
prayer of exorcism:

> Almighty and ever-living God, you sent your
> only Son into the world to cast out the power of
> Satan, spirit of evil, to rescue man from the king-
> dom of darkness, and bring him into the splendor
> of your kingdom of light. We pray for this child:
> set him (her) free from original sin, make him
> (her) a temple of your glory, and send your Holy
> Spirit to dwell with him (her).
>
> (Rite Of Baptism)

Through the indwelling Spirit, infants are joined to the
body of Christ, becoming members of the Christian family

and true children of God the Father. Parents promise to nurture and protect the new divine life within their children throughout their lives, and the priest proclaims "N., the Christian community welcomes you with great joy. In its name I claim you for Christ our Savior by the sign of his cross." Baptized, they will live and mature under the banner of Christ's sacred cross, the means of their salvation and eternal life.

Born Again Of Water And The Spirit

What then is the great work of the Holy Spirit in baptism? Cyril of Jerusalem proclaimed it to his catechumens:

> Great is the baptism that lies before you: a ransom to captives; a remission of offences; a death to sin; a new birth of the soul; a garment of light, a holy indissoluble seal; a chariot to heaven; the delight of Paradise; a welcome into the kingdom; the gift of adoption!
>
> (*Procat.*, 16)

The key to understanding what the Holy Spirit does within us at baptism is to know what the term *to baptize* means. The image it suggests is often lost on contemporary Christians. In Greek, *bapto*—to baptize—means to immerse, to wash or to soak. Early Christians baptized by total immersion in water, a practice some Christian denominations today still observe and which, though rarely done, is also a legitimate option for baptism within the Catholic Church.

Water is an important scriptural symbol of the life and action of the Holy Spirit. Its importance is fully expressed in the Christian rite of baptism, in which the Spirit becomes the river of "living waters" that springs up in human hearts (John 7:38). The image used is Jesus immersing, washing or soaking us in the Holy Spirit. Just as a sponge in water absorbs and becomes entirely filled with water, so we, immersed in the Holy Spirit, absorb (or better, are absorbed by) and become entirely filled with the Spirit. Water also represents a dual effect of immersion in the Holy Spirit. Just as water is used to wash and sustain life, the Spirit washes us clean of sin, and, sanctifies and sustains us in new life by giving himself to us. "You were washed, you were sanctified, you were justified in the name of the Lord Jesus Christ and in the Spirit of our God" (1 Corinthians 6:11).

Thus, through water and Spirit, we are "born again" in baptism to a new life with God (John 3:5). We become new creations through the Spirit. At creation, the Spirit hovered over the waters and God breathed his Spirit into man (Genesis 1:1 and 2:7). So in baptism, the Spirit hovers over new "living waters" and God breathes his Spirit into the believer anew, recreating him. Paul tells Titus that God saved us "by the washing of regeneration and renewal in the Holy Spirit, which he (God) poured out upon us richly through Jesus Christ our Saviour. . ." (Titus 3:5-6). To be born again, justified or regenerated means that, through the Spirit now dwelling in us, we have a new life and relationship with God. We have received the Spirit of adoption, enabling us to cry out, "Abba! Father!" With our fellow believers, we can say, "We are children of God and if children, then heirs, heirs of God and fellow heirs with Christ . . . " (Romans 8:15-17; see Galatians 4:5-7). The Holy Spirit has re-established within us the proper relationship with God as our Father, and thus has sealed us as God's children, guaranteeing our inheritance, eternal life with him (see Ephesians 1:13-14; 2 Corinthians 1:22, 5:5).

The effects of baptism are founded on this fact: by the power of the Spirit, we actually participate in the death and the resurrection of Christ. Jesus died on the cross for our sin and rose to give us new life with God. The Spirit makes these saving mysteries present in baptism, enabling us to participate in them and obtain their benefits. Paul exhorts the Romans,

> Do you not know that all of us who have been baptized into Christ Jesus were baptized into his death? We were buried therefore with him by baptism into death, so that as Christ was raised from the dead by the glory of the Father, we too might walk in newness of life.
>
> (Romans 6:3-4; see Colossians 2:12)

We enter the water and die to sin. We rise from the water to newness of life. Cyril of Jerusalem impresses this truth upon the newly baptized. "O strange and inconceivable thing! We did not really die, we were not really buried, we were not really crucified and raised again· but our imitation was in a figure, and our salvation in reality" (*Myst. Cat.*, 2, 5; see 2, 4-6). For Cyril, our salvation is a reality (even though in baptism we only imitate Christ) because we participate in these mysteries through the work of the Spirit. Baptism completes our transformation from the old fallen life of the flesh to the new risen life of the Spirit.

Baptism contains other symbols of transformation. Clothing with a white garment, for example, shows that we have clothed ourselves in Christ through the purification of the Spirit. "For as many of you as were baptized into Christ have put on Christ" (Galatians 3:27). Anointing with oil indicates that the Father has chosen each of us specifically and sealed us in the Spirit. God anointed priests, prophets and kings in the Old Testament and, afterwards, anointed Jesus as the Messiah. So now he anoints each Christian as a member of his Son's body.

The Spirit is the life in baptism that unites us to Christ and to the other members of his body. "For by one Spirit we were all baptized into one body—Jews or Greeks, slaves or free—and all were made to drink of one Spirit" (1 Corinthians 12:13). The Spirit is the source of all unity. Thus "There is one body and one Spirit . . . one Lord, one faith, one baptism, one God and Father of us all . . ." (Ephesians 4:4-6).

Many of us might not appreciate the great change the Holy Spirit worked in us through baptism or, perhaps, have not experienced its effects in our lives. St. Cyprian of Carthage (d. 258) professes the radical change that occurred in his own life as a result of conversion and baptism.

> I was myself so entangled and constrained by the very many errors of my former life that I could not believe it possible for me to escape from them, so much was I subservient to the faults which clung to me; and in despair of improvement I cherished these evils of mine as if they had been my dearest possessions. But when the stain of my earlier life had been washed away by the help of the water of birth, and light from above had poured down upon my heart, now cleansed and purified; when I had drunk the Spirit from heaven, and the second birth had restored me so as to make me a new man; then straightway in a marvelous manner doubts began to be resolved, closed doors to open, dark places to grow light; what before had seemed difficult was now easy, what I had thought impossible was now capable of accomplishment; so that I could now see that what had been born after the flesh and lived at the mercy of sin belonged to the

> earth, while that which the Holy Spirit was
> enlivening had begun to belong to God.
>
> (*Ad. Don.*, 4)

Each of us should be able to bear witness to such a change
as well. If you have not experienced such a change, ask the
Lord to show you why. The Spirit will reveal to you where
repentance and faith may be necessary. Pray that the work
the Spirit begins at baptism will be completed in you and
that you will be grateful for the gift of the Holy Spirit.

Confirmation

The history and nature of the sacrament of confirmation are rather complex, in part because in the first centuries, baptism and confirmation were segments of a single
liturgical rite. The distinct sacramental aspects of confirmation came clearly into focus in the West only as it was
gradually detached from baptism. Before Vatican II, the
age for reception of the sacrament varied from country to
country. Some children were confirmed in infancy or
between eight and ten years old; others were not confirmed until late adolescence. Currently, the usual age for
confirmation in the Catholic Church in North America is
fourteen to sixteen. The separation never took place in the
Eastern Orthodox Churches and, to this day, children are
baptized and confirmed in the same liturgical rite. The
liturgical unity of these two sacraments has been main-
tained in the West only in the case of adult converts, but
the Second Vatican Council called for revision of the rite
of confirmation so that "the intimate connection of this
sacrament with the whole of the Christian initiation may
more clearly appear" (*S.C.*, 71).

A rather perplexing question surrounds the Holy Spirit and confirmation: how does the Spirit's presence and

action in confirmation differ from those at baptism? The Western church has emphasized, due in part to the later age at which confirmation is received, that in confirmation, the Holy Spirit makes us mature Christians, commissioned to be witnesses to Jesus Christ and the gospel. Despite historical and theological complexities surrounding the sacrament of confirmation, a few essential points are very clear. Confirmation is part of our initiation into the full Christian life. We do receive the Holy Spirit more completely and, because of this, we are called and empowered to live a more mature and holy Christian life. We would like to stress these points here.

Confirmation And The Holy Spirit

The tradition of the Catholic Church states unanimously that the Holy Spirit is imparted in the rite of confirmation. In the third century, Hippolytus described the sequel to the baptismal washing saying,

> The bishop shall lay his hand upon them [the catechumens] invoking and saying: O Lord God, who didst count these worthy of discovering the forgiveness of sins by the laver of regeneration, make them worthy to be filled with thy Holy Spirit and send upon them thy grace, that they may serve thee according to thy will. He then anoints them with "holy oil" and seals them on the forehead with the sign of the cross.
>
> (*Trad. Apost.*, 22, 1-3)

Another prayer, probably originating in the sixth century, was prayed as the bishop signed the forehead with chrism:

> Almighty God, Father of our Lord Jesus Christ, who hast made thy servants to be regenerated of

water and the Holy Spirit, and hast given them remission of all their sins, do thou, Lord send upon them thy Holy Spirit, the Paraclete, and give them the spirit of wisdom and understanding, the spirit of counsel and might, the spirit of knowledge and godliness and fill them with the spirit of the fear of God.

(Rite of Confirmation)

These quotations clearly indicate that the reception of the Holy Spirit is essential to the sacrament of confirmation, a teaching the Catholic Church corroborated both in the Council of Florence (14381445) and the Council of Trent (1545-1563). The present rite of confirmation continues the tradition. The priest anoints our foreheads with the sign of the cross and says simply, "Be sealed with the Holy Spirit, the gift of the Father" *(Rite of Confirmation)*.

Endowed With The Spirit

The laying on of hands and anointing with oil in confirmation complete and perfect the action and presence of the Holy Spirit we receive at baptism. Cyril of Jerusalem states that through the anointing we "have been made Christs" since we possess the Holy Spirit (*Myst. Cat.*, 3, 1; see 3, 2). "While your body is anointed with visible ointment, your soul is sanctified by the holy and life-giving Spirit" (*ibid.*, 3, 3). Confirmation and baptism complement each other, emphasizing the importance of both in the complete initiation process to the full Christian life. This does not mean that having received both sacraments, we are perfect, but that we are now fully equipped with the Spirit's presence and gifts to live out the Christian life and become holy. Though we must still grow in Christian maturity, we have the means to do so at our disposal.

In the Western Church, confirmation is understood primarily as the sacrament in which we receive the power of the Spirit to live and witness to our faith as adult believers. The Holy Spirit we receive enables us to direct our lives according to the life and power of the Spirit within us. We are to live under the convicting power of the Spirit. The chrism (oil) of confirmation makes us "the aroma of Christ to God among those who are being saved and among those who are perishing, to one a fragrance from death to death, to the other a fragrance from life to life" (2 Corinthians 2:15-16). As early as the third century, the church proclaimed,

> For as Christ, after his baptism and the visitation of the Holy Spirit, went forth and vanquished the adversary, so likewise you, after holy baptism and thy mystical chrism, having put on the whole armour of the Holy Spirit, are to stand against the power of the adversary and vanquish it.
>
> (*Myst. Cat.*, 3, 4)

The Spirit commissions us to witness boldly to the gospel, to confess our faith with courage and, if need be, to suffer persecution and martyrdom for the sake of the kingdom. In the past, confirmed Christians were encouraged to be "soldiers of Jesus Christ." Today, the Council Fathers at Vatican II state the Christian calling this way:

> By the sacrament of confirmation they are more perfectly bound to the Church and endowed with the special strength of the Holy Spirit. Hence they are, as true witnesses of Christ, more strictly obliged to spread the faith by word and deed.
>
> (*L.G.*, 11)

Practically and pastorally, however, this understanding of confirmation poses a problem. Many confirmed Christians do not in any real way proclaim or bear witness to the gospel, just as many baptized Christians do not live Christian lives. In the Roman Catholic Church and the Church of England, the problem has been generally addressed by raising the age for confirmation in the hope that those to be confirmed will make a more mature commitment, thus the sacrament will have greater effect. The success of this solution, though, appears limited. The heart of the problem is that apathetic adolescent Christians, like nonpracticing adult Christians, need to hear the gospel proclaimed in an environment where conversion can occur and faith can grow and mature. Otherwise, the sacrament will remain an empty sign with little real effect. Once we experience conversion, however, the grace of confirmation comes to life in us. Having experienced the good news, we will desire to share it with others, which we can do by the power of the Holy Spirit within us.

Most of us have been baptized and confirmed. Having entered into the body of Christ, we are called to be servants within that body. The glorious Lord acted in these sacraments by the power of the Holy Spirit to work great changes in us. Yet many of us have barely tapped the boundless power of the Holy Spirit who dwells within us. God is calling us to be faithful to our baptismal promises, to reject sin, to commit our lives to Christ. He is urging us to be witnesses and heralds of the gospel. Paul counsels us, "Do not grieve the Holy Spirit of God, in whom you were sealed for the day of redemption" (Ephesians 4:30).

Chapter Eight

The Holy Spirit
And The Body Of Christ

AS WE EXPERIENCE CONVERSION, WE ARE INCORPO-
rated into the living body of Jesus Christ on
earth. We leave the kingdom of darkness. Cleansing from sin and new life of the Spirit graft us
into the fellowship of believers, the body of Christ. In the
third Eucharistic prayer, Catholics pray that they "may be
filled with the Holy Spirit and become one body, one Spirit
in Christ." Because of the fall, each of us must individually
accept salvation in Jesus Christ. Yet in conversion, the
Spirit is never concerned with us as isolated individuals.
Rather, he always works to join us to the one people of
God. Conversion by necessity brings us into the body of
Christ, for such was God's plan from the beginning of
time. Above all else, he desired a people he could call his
own (see Genesis 12:2; Deuteronomy 7:7-9; Jeremiah 31:1,
33), which he ultimately accomplished through the death
and resurrection of his Son. This chapter discusses both
the communal aspect of conversion and our entrance into
the body of Christ as it is fully expressed in the liturgy of
the eucharist.

Baptized By One Spirit Into One Body

St. Paul writes to the Corinthians, "By one Spirit we were all baptized into one body—Jews or Greeks, slave or free, and all were made to drink of one Spirit" (1 Corinthians 12:13). God establishes us, through faith, in a relationship with his Son, Jesus, giving us a relationship with all believers. We all share the same Spirit, and have all been "called in the one body" (Colossians 3:15). The Holy Spirit's work in conversion to bring us into the one body is illustrated in the event of Pentecost. According to Luke, the Holy Spirit came upon the assembled body of apostles and there appeared "tongues as of fire, distributed and resting on each one of them" (Acts 2:3). The tongues of fire, distributed individually, find their source in the Holy Spirit. He fills all of us individually, while uniting us to himself and to one another.

The unity the Holy Spirit brings was also manifested at Pentecost when each Jew, whether from Mesopotamia, Pontus or Asia, heard the apostles speaking "in his own language" (Acts 2:8). For Luke, the story of the tower of Babel is reversed by the outpouring of the Holy Spirit at Pentecost (see Genesis 11:1-9). Sin destroyed the unity of mankind but the Holy Spirit restores the brotherhood God intended for his people from the beginning. When we accept Jesus as Lord, we can be united with others, who become our true brothers and sisters. Thus, following Peter's Pentecost sermon and the baptism of the first converts, Luke tells us:

> They devoted themselves to the apostles' teaching and fellowship, to the breaking of bread and the prayers . . . and all who believed were together and had all things in common; and they sold their

possessions and goods and distributed them all,
as any had need.

(*Acts 2:42, 44-45*)

Fellowship, the natural response to receiving the Holy
Spirit in conversion, results when we concretely live out
the unity established by the Spirit of Christ. As the Holy
Spirit binds us to Christ and other Christians, community
becomes an essential and integral part of our Christian
lives. The Second Vatican Council states,

> Giving the body unity through himself, both by
> his own power and by the interior union of the
> members, this same Spirit produces and stimu-
> lates love among the faithful. From this it follows
> that if one member suffers anything, all the mem-
> bers suffer with him, and if one member is hon-
> ored, all the members together rejoice (see 1 Corin
> thians 12:26).

(*L.G., 7*)

The Spirit Gives Life To Christ's Body

Paul is the theologian of the body of Christ. Throughout
Paul's teaching is the truth that the Spirit brings about
unity and gives life and growth to the body. Paul develops
this theology throughout 1 Corinthians, especially in chapter twelve where he states that we are baptized into one
body by one Spirit (see 1 Corinthians 12:13). Paul urges us
to be eager to "maintain the unity of the Spirit in the bond
of peace" (Ephesians 4:3), which is such a high priority
because "there is one body and one Spirit" (Ephesians 4:4).
"For as in one body we have many members, and all the
members do not have the same function, so we, though
many, are one body in Christ, and individually members
one of another (Romans 12:4-5).

In Romans and Corinthians, Paul stresses our unity with one another in Christ through the Spirit. In Ephesians, however, his emphasis changes: Christ is the head and we are the body united to the head. "Christ is the head of the church, his body, and is himself its Savior" (Ephesians 5:23; see also Ephesians 1:10, 22; 4:15). To function properly, the body must rely on the Spirit's life and power as directed by Jesus Christ the Lord, who empowers and governs the members of his body through the Spirit, so that they live and act as one.

Paul's image of the body of Christ is not just an illustration or metaphor. The Holy Spirit is vital and effective. So, too, the one body of Christ he forms is concrete and real. The community of Christians actually does become one living reality in Christ through the Spirit. Paul describes a fact: christians share a common life with and under Christ in the Holy Spirit.

The unity of Christians through the Holy Spirit is described in a distinctive way in John's Gospel, where Jesus says, "I am the vine, you are the branches. He who abides in me and I in him, he it is that bears much fruit, for apart from me you can do nothing" (John 15:5). The witness of tradition, and Paul's teaching on the body of Christ, show us that the life of the Holy Spirit is what grafts us onto Christ. The life that flows from him, enabling us to live and bear fruit, is that same life of the Holy Spirit.

Jesus prays for us that we "may all be one; even as thou, Father, art in me, and I in thee, that they also may be in us, so that the world may believe that thou hast sent me" (John 17:21). Our unity of one with another and with the Father and the Son can only be achieved in and through the Spirit. The Spirit is the bond of life and love that makes the Father and the Son one, and unifies and unites us to the Father and the Son. Commenting on John's Gospel,

Cyril of Alexandria stresses that

> The mystery of Christ is available for us as a beginning and a way for our participation in the Holy Spirit, and our union with God. . . . We all receive the one same Spirit, the Holy Spirit, and thus are mingled, as it were, with one another with God . . .
>
> (In Joh., 17, 21, see John 1:14)

Recognizing The Truth Of Christ's Body

The communal nature of conversion is not a side-effect, but the very essence of conversion. It is important in our contemporary Christian situation, and something we must keep in mind for ourselves, our children and all to whom we proclaim the gospel. It needs to be emphasized because so often today we hear expressions like, "Religion is a personal thing," "My faith is solely between God and me," "My faith is strictly my private domain. What I believe is not the concern of others." We can be deceived by such erroneous thinking, seeing our faith as a purely private affair between ourselves and God.

If we are comfortable with "where we are," we might think that no one should try to tell us any different, nor should we be expected to make any personal contribution to building up the larger body of Christ. Thus we fail to recognize that each Christian has a responsibility for the well-being and salvation of other Christians, and we live our "Christian" lives in isolation from fellow Christians. This isolation leads to a defective experience of Christianity, even though we might be unable to perceive that something is seriously lacking. When we truly know Jesus Christ and have a living experience of Christ's body, however, the negative effects of such isolation are all too obvious. We must realize that when Jesus founded the church, he intended it to be his living body of believers bound together in love and care for each other.

Children are also prey to this type of thinking about isolation. They might reason that as long as they are "good" and go to Mass on Sunday, they are doing all that is expected of them, not grasping that they are brothers and sisters in the Lord with other believers. They might fail to realize Christianity is a way of life that involves more than themselves, their family and God, and remain oblivious to the reality of Christ's living body in which, as adults, they will be called to play an integral and responsible role. Mature Christian parents, by living with and relating to other Christians, can help their children learn that to be a Christian is to be part of the people of God who must love, care and be responsible for the life and salvation of their Christian brothers and sisters.

What does it mean to live as Christian brothers and sisters? Practical ways to establish Christian fellowship in our own families include family prayer before dinner or conversation about specific scripture passages. Family prayer and scripture study allow parents to teach their children the faith and encourage them to live virtuous lives. Baptisms, first confessions, first communions, confirmations, weddings and funerals are also good times to discuss the gospel as it applies to these concrete events in the life of the family. Another practical example of fostering Christian fellowship would be for two or three families to come together at regular, set times to pray. Even if the children are not included every time, it is a good witness that also provides mutual support and care to the parents of the individual families. Together, they can foster their relationship with Christ and seek his wisdom.

This type of Christian fellowship can be organized in the parish or, less formally, among families that come together because of their desire to share their lives with other Christians. Relating and caring for one another means more than communal prayer or discussion of scripture. It also means that we forgive one another rather than hold grudges and resentments, and that we ask forgiveness when we offend others rather than pass it off, hoping they will forget. (They usually don't.) Being brothers and sisters in Christ means that, when we have problems, concerns and differences, we work out solutions instead of "writing off" each other. Christian fellowship demands that our conversations with one another go deeper than discussions of the weather and sports to include common Christian concerns, what we think God is saying to us and our families, how he wants us to change and grow. Christian friendship takes time and honest effort but, with humility, openness and commitment, the Holy Spirit can build up close Christian fellowship.

The best indicator of whether or not we are seeking to live as brothers and sisters is our willingness to discuss our personal and Christian lives with one another. Are we open with one another? Can we discuss the gospel and how it affects our lives? Can we pray simply with one another? Can spouses pray together and with their children? Do we have friends with whom we can pray?

The Eucharist:
Sacrament Of The Spirit's Unity

We are baptized into the one body of Christ, which is visibly expressed in our communion in the eucharist.

> The cup of blessing which we bless, is it not a participation in the blood of Christ? The bread which we break, is it not a participation in the body of Christ? Because there is one bread, we

who are many are one body, for we all partake of
the one bread.

(*1 Corinthians 10:16-17*)

The eucharist is the principal sign and source of unity
among believers. The Council Fathers at Vatican II stressed
that the eucharist is the culmination of the church's apostolic activity. Those who hear the word of God, believe
and are baptized in water and in Spirit, come together in
unity and fellowship to participate in the saving mystery
of the cross and to partake of the Lord's banquet:

> The liturgy is the summit towards which the
> activity of the church is directed; it is also the
> fount from which all her power flows. For the
> goal of apostolic endeavour is that all who are
> made sons of God by faith and baptism should
> come together to praise God in the midst of his
> church, to take part in the sacrifice and to eat the
> Lord's supper.
>
> (*S.C.*, 10)

The early church saw participation in the eucharist as
the crowning achievements of conversion. Ambrose tells
us, "Rich with these adornments (baptism and confirmation) the cleansed people hasten to the altar of Christ" (*De
Myst.*, 8, 43). The Eastern Churches today still give holy
communion to newly baptized and confirmed infants, reasoning in faith that even they, baptized in water and sealed
with the Spirit, can legitimately and fully participate in the
body of Christ's greatest act of worship of the Father. The
Spirit's action in baptism initiates us into the life of the
Trinity. Simultaneously, we enter the fellowship of Chris-

tians so that, filled with the Spirit and incorporated into the body, we can worship the Father "in Spirit and in truth" (John 4:23), in union with our brothers and sisters in Christ.

The eucharist expresses the unity achieved among Christians through the Spirit and serves as the Spirit's instrument to foster unity. Augustine expressed it in the fifth century, saying, "The spiritual benefit there (in the eucharist) understood is unity, that being joined to his body and made his members we may be what we receive," that is, the full and mature body of Christ (Serm., 57, 7). The Vatican II Fathers proclaim the same thing today, "In the sacrament of the eucharistic bread, the unity of believers, who form one body in Christ, is both expressed and brought about" (L.G., 3; see 7, 11, 26).

In the eucharist, the Holy Spirit enables God's people to participate in and benefit from Christ's death and resurrection. Though Jesus died two thousand years ago, "one for all" (Hebrews 10:10), the Holy Spirit makes these saving mysteries present today through the eucharist liturgy, so that persons of every age can unite themselves to Christ on the cross and rise to new life in him. We, the body of Christ, do not just remember the past great deeds of Christ, we actually become one with his sacrifice on the cross. With Christ, we offer ourselves to the Father as an atonement for sin and become a living sacrifice of praise, having been cleansed of sin by his blood (see Hebrews 9:14). In turn, the Father pours his love into our hearts through Christ so that we come to share in his resurrected life by the power of the Holy Spirit.

The Holy Spirit also transforms the bread and wine into the reality of Christ's resurrected body and blood, the very person of Jesus our Lord. Those who receive communion have the glorious Savior dwelling within them, and, moreover, are being united to Christ and one another in a deeper way. Thus we see that our conversion is conversion into the body of Christ. This truth is expressed in the liturgy, where we ask in the second eucharistic prayer, "May all of us who share in the body and blood of Christ be brought together in unity by the Holy Spirit." (See also the third eucharistic prayer.) As we partake of Jesus' body and blood, he builds, molds and nourishes us, who are his body, through his resurrected life in the Holy Spirit. We become one with him and, with him, one with one another. Receiving Christ himself, we become living members of his one body. Paul states emphatically, "Because there is one bread, we who are many are one body, for we all partake of the one bread" (1 Corinthians 19:17).

Thus, for Paul, partaking of Christ's body and blood without recognizing the body of believers who offer it and are formed by it is a grave sin with dire consequences. "Any one who eats and drinks without discerning the body eats and drinks judgment upon himself. That is why many of you are weak and ill, and some have died" (1 Corinthians 11:29-30). When we participate in the eucharist and then offend God by sinning against the brethren, we destroy the reality the Spirit has formed in making us the body of Christ. In the eucharist, we experience the present unity of Christ's body and so enjoy a foretaste of the heavenly banquet. Right here and now, the Spirit makes the future present. The heavenly reality already at hand! In the liturgy, we gather in the unity of the Holy Spirit before the eternal throne of the Father to be a living sacrifice of praise. The priest prays that all may come to share fully in the company of the angels and saints: "Then, in your kingdom, freed from the corruption of sin and death, we shall sing your glory with every creature through Christ our Lord. . . ." (*Fourth Eucharistic Prayer*).

The Eucharist And Conversion

Many of us who are older can vividly remember the changes in the liturgy brought about by the Second Vatican Council. These changes were the most visible expression of the Council's work, which was to renew the liturgy. The eucharist began to be celebrated in our vernacular, congregational participation through song was expressed and altars were turned around. These good and wise changes were made under the inspiration of the Holy Spirit. The changes in the liturgy, however, have not brought about the renewal the Council Fathers hoped for—Sunday Masses are not filled with vibrant worshippers.

Many people attend Mass faithfully each Sunday, yet come ignorant of what is taking place, lacking interest or lacking faith in God and his salvation. We might even be angry with God because of situations in our lives, or our minds might be focused on other things like work, family and plans for the day. We might complain of being bored and not "getting anything out of the Mass." Some of us might be critical (sometimes validly) of uninspiring, trite homilies. Negative feelings toward the Mass often run deeper in our children, especially teenagers. Frequently, we have to argue with them to make them come. "Guitar Masses," "youth Masses" or other enticements we might offer highlight rather than solve the problem. Many priests, religion teachers and parents raise their hands in despair and say, "We just can't reach them." Actually, though, something is missing at a deeper level.

Better-executed, more creative liturgies or just the right young celebrant who can relate to our children are obviously important and advantageous, but will not solve the basic problem. The heart of the problem is not knowing Christ. The solution lies only in conversion! Until we are converted to Jesus Christ, the liturgy will not touch our lives. We gather as God's people to worship him only when we have come to true repentance and mature faith. We appreciate the Mass when we pray daily, read scripture and examine our consciences. We will desire to come together as Christ's body if we strive each day to keep his commandments, care for his people and live out our responsibilities as Christian men and women. In other words, the Mass will become meaningful to us when we begin truly to live the Christian life. Until then, the liturgy remains, for the most part, an empty ritual.

Priests, teachers and parents must remember this truth. When we see others failing to appreciate the Mass, we immediately think we must teach them more about it. So we provide special lectures and more courses—and very little happens. Neither adults nor children will recognize the marvelous gift of the eucharist merely by learning more about it. We must begin by proclaiming and teaching the basic truths of the gospel. Starting with the basics is a fundamental rule of education. If students are to appreciate Bach, for example, the music professor does not start with Bach. It would be impossible for them to grasp such intricate music. The teacher begins with the rudiments of music and builds up. The same is true for the liturgy. We, especially children and and non-practicing Christians, must begin by learning the basic truths of our faith: God created us, we sinned and Jesus died for us. We must learn to pray, repent and obey God each day. Knowing the facts, though essential, is not enough. We have had classes and courses on Jesus, the bible and the sacraments, yet we do not necessarily live what we have been taught. We must come to the point where such truths as the fall, Jesus' divinity and God's love are realities that actually affect how we live. The gospel must penetrate how we think and act.

Children might need years of parents' and teachers' constant attention and work before the truths become realities. As adults, we must consistently work at "living by faith" and not by our sinful nature. Only when we begin to see a need for Jesus, to desire his salvation and eternal life, and to glimpse the Father's love, will we want to worship the Father with Christ in the eucharist.

This obviously does not mean that children and lukewarm Christians should stay away from Sunday Mass. We should all go and be encouraged to participate. Participation will aid our conversion. The key to understanding and appreciating the liturgy, however, is ongoing conversion and living the Christian life. While the eucharist is the summit of Catholic worship, it must be placed within, for it only makes sense within the truths of the gospel lived out in the Spirit. Catholics who live the Christian life in humble repentance and vibrant faith will worship the Father with Christ in spirit and in truth (see John 4:23).

The Father has given us a marvelous gift by incorporating us into the body of his eternal Son, and we should thank him for the great privilege of having brothers and sisters in Christ. We need to pray, too, that we will see and understand more clearly the precious truth that in the eucharist we receive Jesus himself and in him are taken, all together, before the heavenly throne of the Father as his sons and daughters. We must know that when we come together, we do so in remembrance of Jesus himself.

The church has always prized the eucharist and emphasized its value, yet today few of us truly honor and cherish it as we ought. Only when our hearts are converted to Christ and our minds are enlightened by the Spirit will we be able to worship the Father. We must pray for that conversion. We must strive for it in our own lives, our families' lives and in the lives of all God's people.

Chapter Nine

Conversion Is No Mystery

WE HAVE SEEN HOW ABSOLUTELY ESSENTIAL CON-version is for every one of us. Conversion is not hard to understand. It is not beyond our comprehension. Conversion is simply coming to new life within the Trinity through repentance for sin and faith in the gospel. It is the beginning of a whole new life in Christ brought about through faith and the Holy Spirit. Conversion is the most marvelous gift God the Father can give to us, for it establishes an entirely new relationship of love with God himself. This gift alone leads to eternal life and finds its fulfillment there. No other gift of God changes our lives so radically and beneficially, no other gift has such a lasting effect.

Because conversion is so valuable a gift, we should cherish it as no other. It is our greatest treasure and should be the most affectionate love of our hearts. Jesus taught his followers the significance of conversion into the kingdom of God:

> The kingdom of heaven is like treasure hidden in a field, which a man found and covered up; then in his joy he goes and sells all that he has and

> buys that field. Again, the kingdom of heaven is
> like a merchant in search of fine pearls, who, on
> finding one pearl of great value, went and sold all
> that he had and bought it.
>
> (*Matthew 13:44-45*)

When we experience the Holy Spirit bringing us to repentance and faith, and our hearts begin to burn at hearing the gospel, we should rejoice and be glad (see Luke 24:32). God is offering us his most valued treasure. He is holding out to us the priceless pearl, and we should never become complacent or take such a great gift for granted. We should instead reverence the work of God in our lives, and protect the transformation that the Spirit has begun in us. Of all the gifts and accomplishments we may take pride in, God's gift of conversion to Christ is the one we must prize above all. We should seek to have the mind of St. Paul, who says,

> But whatever gain I had, I counted as loss for the
> sake of Christ. Indeed I count everything as loss
> because of the surpassing worth of knowing
> Christ Jesus my Lord. For his sake I have suf-
> fered the loss of all things, and count them as
> refuse, in order that I may gain Christ.
>
> (*Philippians 3:7-8*)

In the parable of the seed, Jesus says that the word of God can fall along the path or upon rocky ground, grow up among thorns and thistles or can mature on good soil. We should seek to be the good soil, for we know the significance of this parable:

> When any one hears the word of the kingdom
> and does not understand it, the evil one comes
> and snatches away what is sown in his heart; this

is what was sown along the path. As for what was sown on rocky ground, this is he who hears the word and immediately receives it with joy; yet he has no root in himself, but endures for a while, and when tribulation or persecution arises on account of the word, immediately he falls away. As for what was sown among thorns, this is he who hears the word, but the cares of the world and the delight in riches choke the word, and it proves unfruitful. As for what was sown on good soil, this is he who hears the word and understands it; he indeed bears fruit, and yields, in one case a hundredfold, in another sixty, and in another thirty.

(Matthew 13:19-23)

Conversion is essential to our life with God, thus we should never think of it as just an isolated occurence that can be over and done with. At one particular point in time, by God's grace, we can experience true conversion. In addition, we need on-going conversion and growth in the Spirit. Here on earth, we can never realize completely the goal of conversion, which is life with God, for the Spirit always wishes to reveal to us more of the Father's love. He ever desires to convict us of sin so we can be purified and recreated into the perfect image of Christ himself.

The Holy Spirit wants to strengthen us in faith and urge us on in hope, to nourish us to love God and one another more deeply every day of our lives. The Holy Spirit wants to bring to completion the work the Father has begun in us through Christ Jesus (see Philippians 1:6). The on-going work of the Holy Spirit, however, requires active cooperation and attentive vigilance. Right now can be a real time of anointing by the Holy Spirit. Now can be a true moment of conversion. The Spirit can empower us to make a deeper commitment to Jesus. With this expectation, let us make the following act of consecration to God on our own behalf and on behalf of the entire world.

Prayer Of Consecration

Father, Son and Holy Spirit, I dedicate my life to you. I humble myself before you. I acknowledge the truth that I am a sinner. My rebelliousness, stubbornness and hardness of heart bear witness to the fact that I neither deserve your love nor long for your mercy. Yet God, all holy Father, your love for me and for the world far exceeds my own callous sin. You sent your Son to us who were your enemies, not to condemn us as we deserve, but to make us holy once more. Father, your Son Incarnate became man, suffered and died for me. He took my sin upon himself. Jesus died as a sacrifice of praise and you, Father, raised him gloriously from the grave. He sits at your right hand in splendor. From there Father, he pours out his Spirit upon the face of the world. He offers the human race new life in the Spirit. He presents eternal life with him to us. He calls us from our isolation to new life in Him.

O Father, I believe in your Son Jesus. I give him my life. I entrust my very being to him. Jesus, my Lord and my God, I humbly accept your gift of salvation. I will be your faithful servant. I will obey you and the Father. I bend my knee before you and give you sole authority over my heart and mind. I give absolute allegiance to no other power or authority on earth, above the earth or below the earth. You are Lord! Holy Spirit purify me of sin. Wash me clean. Soften my hard heart. Pierce the darkness of my mind. Make me holy. Seal me in redemption. Be my hope of resurrection and my guarantee of eternal life.

Father, Son and Holy Spirit, I love you with all my heart, mind and strength. Help me to love my brothers and sisters. Help me to lay down my life for their salvation. I dedicate the whole world, all of mankind to you. I repent on behalf of us all for not giving you, blessed Trinity, the glory you alone deserve. Trinity of love, Trinity of life, look upon your people with mercy. Let not the hatred we bear to one another and the indifference we show to you end in our destruction. I call upon your faithfulness and kindness. I entrust to you the salvation of all. There is no other to whom we can turn. In you alone is our hope.

I promise, Father, Son and Holy Spirit, to live and to proclaim the gospel to your glory and honor forever and ever. Amen."

Bibliography

Quotations in this book are taken from the following works.

Anselm, St., *Basic Writings,* trans. S.N. Deane, La Salle, Illinois: Open Court, 1966
> *Trinity, Incarnation and Redemption, Theological Treatise,* ed. J. Hopkins and H. Richardson, New York: Harper Torchbooks, 1970.

Augustine, St., *Basic Writings,* ed. Whitney J. Oates, New York: Random House, 1948.

Basil the Great, St., *On The Holy Spirit,* Crestwood, New York: St. Vladimir's Press, 1980.

Bettenson, H., ed. and trans., *The Early Christian Fathers,* Oxford: Oxford Universtiy Press, 1956.
> *The Later Christian Fathers,* Oxford: Oxford University Press, 1956.

Clarkson, J.F., *et al.,* ed., *The Church Teaches,* St. Louis: Herder, 1957.

Deiss, Lucien, *Early Sources of the Liturgy,* Staten Island: Alba House, 1967.

Denzinger/Schonmetzer, *Enchiridion Symbolorum Definitionum Et Declarationum,* ed. XXVI, Freiburg: Herder, 1973.

Flannery, A., ed., *Vatican Council II: The Conciliar and Post-Conciliar Documents,* Northport, New York: Costello Publishing Co., 1975.

Habig, M.A., ed., *St. Francis of Assisi: Omnibus of Sources,* Chicago: Franciscan Herald Press, 1972.

John of Avila, St., *The Holy Ghost*, Chicago: Scepter, 1959.

John Paul II, *Reconciliata et Paenitentia (On Reconciliation and Penance)*, Boston: Daughters of St. Paul, 1984.

Mottola, A., *et al.*, *The Spiritual Exercises of St. Ignatius*, Garden City, New Jersey: Doubleday, Image Books, 1964.

Paul VI, *Evangelii Nuntiandi (On Evangelization in the Modern World)*, Washington, DC: United States Catholic Conference, 1975.

About The Publisher

THE WORD AMONG US PRESS IS AN ORGANIZATION formed to proclaim the gospel message in order to lead people to Christ. Its principal publication is a monthly magazine, *The Word Among Us*, designed to serve as a daily guide to the Christian life, helping individuals and families through daily prayer and Scripture reading.

The Word Among Us is written and published by members of the Mother of God Community, consisting of some 1200 members, both lay and religious, located in the Washington, D.C. area. The writing is done chiefly by a team of priests and scholars who have extensive training and experience in biblical studies, church history, christology, canon law and theology. In addition, they have vast experience in counseling and pastoral guidance. Because it is the product of a lived-out Christianity, *The Word Among Us* is able to deal with the principles of faith in actual practice. By faithfully proclaiming the gospel message, *The Word Among Us* has brought people to a deeper knowledge of Jesus Christ and a more effective response to him.

Subscription rate is $15.00 per year. Write to **The Word Among Us**, *P.O. Box 3646, Washington, D.C. 20007 for details.*